THE MARY SURRATT "LINCOLN ASSASSINATION" TRIAL

A Headline Court Case

Headline Court Cases

THE
MARY SURRATT
"LINCOLN ASSASSINATION"
TRIAL

A Headline Court Case

Bryna J. Fireside

Mrs MARY E. SURRATT

Enslow Publishers, Inc.

40 Industrial Road   PO Box 38
Box 398   Aldershot
Berkeley Heights, NJ 07922   Hants GU12 6BP
USA   UK

http://www.enslow.com

Dedicated to Laura Weeldreyer

Library of Congress Cataloging-in-Publication Data

Fireside, Bryna J.

The Mary Surratt "Lincoln assassination" trial : a headline court case / Bryna J.
Fireside.
p. cm. — (Headline court cases)
Includes bibliographical references and index.
ISBN 0-7660-1481-9
1. Surratt, Mary E. (Mary Eugenia), 1820–1865—Trials, litigation, etc.—Juvenile
literature. 2. Lincoln, Abraham, 1809–1865—Assassination—Juvenile literature.
3. Trials (Assassination)—Washington (D.C.)—Juvenile literature. I. Title. II. Series.
KF224.S79 F57 2000
973.7'092—dc21
                00-010679

Printed in the United States of America

10 9 8 7 6 5 4 3 2 1

To Our Readers:
All Internet Addresses in this book were active and appropriate when we went to press.
Any comments or suggestions can be sent by e-mail to Comments@enslow.com or to
the address on the back cover.

Photo Credits: Courtesy National Archives, Brady Collection, *Dictionary of
American Portraits*, Dover Publications, Inc., © 1967, p. 61; Courtesy National
Park Service, p. 22; Courtesy Surratt House Museum, pp, 3, 9, 15, 16, 18, 20,
29, 31, 36, 41, 50, 52, 54, 58, 66, 71, 84, 96, 97; National Archives, pp. 25, 27,
37, 101; Retouched photograph by Matthew Brady, Courtesy U.S. Department
of State, *Dictionary of American Portraits*, Dover Publications, Inc., © 1967,
p. 47.

Cover Photo: Courtesy Surratt House Museum

Contents

Acknowledgments

There are so many people who freely gave of their time to make this book possible. Everyone who is associated with the Surratt House Museum spent a great deal of time gathering material for me during the several days I spent going through their archives. They were also very gracious in answering questions by phone as I began to organize my notes for the actual writing of this book. Many thanks to Laurie Verge, director of The Surratt House Museum, Joan Chaconas, program assistant, and Margery Patten, administrative aide.

Thank you to James O. Hall, who is a leading authority on the Lincoln assassination. He spent an entire afternoon with me, sharing documents he has patiently collected over the years.

I am also grateful to Olin Library at Cornell University for its outstanding collection of books on the Lincoln assassination, and to the reference librarians at the Tompkins County Library. Thanks also go to Jack Goldman, owner of The Bookery, who was able to find several out-of-print books for me.

Robert V. S. Norton, whose Web site I discovered, was especially helpful with Chapter 3 about Lincoln's enemies.

And finally, thanks to my husband, Harvey Fireside, who always helps me with all the nitty-gritty work such as glossaries, indexes, spelling, and scouting out some of the best sources. Many thanks to all of these wonderful people.

Who's Who in the Lincoln Assassination

The assassination of President Abraham Lincoln in 1865 sent the United States into deep mourning. People wanted those who were responsible for this terrible deed punished, and punished quickly. Here are the people involved in the assassination and in the trial of the conspirators.

- Federick Aiken—Attorney for Mary Surratt.

- Samuel Arnold—Defendant in trial.

- George Atzerodt—Defendant in trial.

- Colonel Lafayette C. Baker—Led the cavalry that captured David Herold and John Wilkes Booth at Garrett's farm.

- Congressman John Bingham—Prosecutor.

- John Wilkes Booth—Shot and killed President Lincoln.

- H. L. Burnett—Prosecutor.

- George Calvert—Mary Surratt owed him five hundred dollars.

- John Clampitt—Attorney for Mary Surratt.

- Boston Corbett—Said to have fired the shot that killed John Wilkes Booth.

- Richard Garrett—Owned the farm where John Wilkes Booth and David Herold hid.

- General Ulysses S. Grant—Was supposed to go to the theater with his wife and the Lincolns on the night of the assassination, but changed his mind.

- Clara Harris—Fiancée of Major Rathbone, also at the theater with the Lincolns.

- David Herold—Defendant in trial.

- Judge Advocate John Holt—Main prosecutor.

- Susan Jackson—Mary Surratt's servant who testified against her.

- J.Z. Jenkins—Brother of Mary Surratt.

- Andrew Johnson—Vice president of the United States under Lincoln, who became president after Lincoln's death.

- Senator Reverdy Johnson—Attorney for Mary Surratt.

- General Robert E. Lee—Southern general who surrendered to General Ulysses S. Grant at the end of the Civil War.

- President Abraham Lincoln—The sixteenth president of the United States who was shot and killed while attending the theater on April 14, 1865.

- Mary Todd Lincoln—Wife of Abraham Lincoln.

The ring of conspirators in the murder of President Lincoln is shown here. John Wilkes Booth (top left) was killed following the assassination, so he was never put on trial.

- John Lloyd—Rented the Surratt Tavern from Mary Surratt. Testified against her.

- Dr. Lewis McMillan—Reported that he knew where John Surratt, Jr. was hiding.

- Dr. Samuel Mudd—Defendant in trial.

- John Nothey—Owed Mary Surratt nearly five hundred dollars.

- Emma Offut—Worked in Surratt Tavern. Testified for Mary Surratt.

- Michael O'Laughlen—Defendant in trial.

- Lewis Paine (a.k.a. Lewis Payne, Lewis Wood)—Tried to kill Secretary of State William Seward.

- Benn Pitman—Official court reporter.

- Major Henry R. Rathbone—Accompanied President and Mrs. Lincoln to the theater on April 14.

- William Henry Seward—Secretary of State.

- Edman Spangler—Defendant in conspiracy trial. (His name is also listed as Edward Spangler in some sources.)

- Edwin Stanton—Secretary of War.

- Anna Surratt—Daughter of Mary Surratt.

- Isaac Surratt—Mary Surratt's oldest son. Was a Confederate soldier in Texas.

- John Surratt, Jr.—Mary Surratt's son. Was a spy for the South. Named as coconspirator in Lincoln assassination. Fled first to Canada, then to England and Italy.

- John Surratt, Sr.—Husband of Mary Surratt.

- Mary Surratt—Owned the Surratt Tavern in Surrattsville, Maryland, and ran a boardinghouse on H Street in Washington, D.C. A defendant in the conspiracy trial.

- Louis J. Weichmann—Lived in Mary Surratt's boardinghouse. Testified against her.

- Reverend B. F. Wiget—Testified for Mary Surratt

- Andrew Wylie—Judge who issued a writ of *habeas corpus* for Mary Surratt.

chapter one

A PRESIDENT IS ASSASSINATED

WASHINGTON, D.C.—On the evening of April 14, 1865, President Abraham Lincoln and his wife, Mary Todd Lincoln, attended a show at Ford's Theatre in Washington, D.C. They were accompanied by friends, Major Henry R. Rathbone and Rathbone's fiancée, Clara Harris. It was the first time in many months that the president and his wife had had an opportunity to enjoy an evening out.

Just four days earlier, the Civil War, which had divided the North and South for the past four years, ended when General Robert E. Lee, commander of the Confederate Army, surrendered to General Ulysses S. Grant, commander of the Union Army, at Appomattox, Virginia.

The Civil War was the bloodiest war in the history of the United States. More than 600,000 men died in battle. This is almost as many Americans as were killed in the Revolutionary War (1775–1783), the War of 1812 (1812–1815), the Mexican War (1846–1848), World War I (1917–1918),

World War II (1941–1945), the Korean Conflict (1950–1953), the Vietnam War (1964–1975), and the Persian Gulf War (1991)—combined.[1]

The end of the Civil War brought four days of celebrations in the nation's capital, and throughout the United States. There were parades in Washington, D.C. Thousands of people were out in the streets celebrating the war's end. People decorated their windows and doorways with the American flag. Stores and schools were closed, but all the taverns and saloons were open. People were joyously toasting the Union's victory over the Confederacy—and the end to the bloodshed.

The United States would never again be divided: Once joined to the Union, a state could not secede (break away). Slavery was forever abolished throughout the nation. The eleven Confederate states—Alabama, Arkansas, Florida, Georgia, Louisiana, Mississippi, North Carolina, South Carolina, Tennessee, Texas, and Virginia—would again become part of the United States. It would be "one nation, indivisible" for all time. President Lincoln was known to favor restoring national harmony rather than punishing the South for the rebellion.

Not Everyone Is Pleased at the War's Outcome

Yet there were many Confederates and Confederate sympathizers in the capital (and elsewhere) who refused to display the American flag. They would take no part in the celebrations. Mary Surratt, a widow who owned a boardinghouse at 541 H Street in Washington, D.C., was one of them. Her oldest son, Isaac, was a Confederate soldier fighting in Texas. Her youngest son, John Surratt, Jr. was a spy for the Confederacy.[2] Mary Surratt had owned slaves before the war. She also owned the Surratt Tavern located in Surrattsville, Maryland, about twelve miles from Washington. Her tavern was a meeting place for Confederate messengers and spies. And in her Washington home, her son John and his friends, including John Wilkes Booth, had once plotted to kidnap President Lincoln, so that they could exchange him for Confederate soldiers who were being held in Northern prisons.[3]

Mary Surratt's boardinghouse was not far from Ford's Theatre, and John Surratt, Jr. and his friends went there often. Surratt's daughter, Anna, especially enjoyed going to the theater when John Wilkes Booth was in a play. Booth was a handsome young actor, from one of the most famous theatrical families in America at the time. He was also a strong supporter of the Confederacy, although he never fought in the war. He was a frequent visitor to the Surratts' boardinghouse. Anna kept a photograph of John Wilkes Booth hidden behind a picture on the mantel of her mother's boardinghouse. (This photograph would later play a part in her mother's arrest.)

The Assassin Takes Deadly Aim

Almost every seat in Ford's Theatre was filled on the night of April 14 because the Washington newspapers advertised that President Lincoln and his wife, and General Ulysses S. Grant and his wife, would be attending the performance.

Many people wanted to see the victorious general and the president.

However, General Grant and his wife decided at the last minute not to attend the play. The Grants went instead by train to visit their children in Burlington, New Jersey. Friends of the president's, Major Rathbone and his fiancée, accompanied the president and Mrs. Lincoln to Ford's Theatre in place of the Grants.[4]

The play, an English comedy called "Our American Cousin," was light and humorous. As the audience laughed at one of the jokes, John Wilkes Booth, who had hidden behind the door which separated him from President Lincoln, pulled out his gun—a

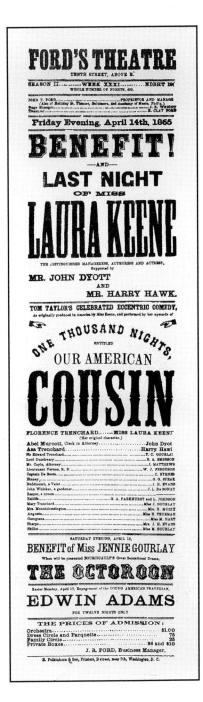

This replica of the playbill announced the showing of "Our American Cousin" at Ford's Theatre.

derringer—opened the door, walked up behind the president, and fired.

President Lincoln was shot at point blank range. Later it would be learned that Booth had been in the Ford's Theatre earlier in the day when Edman Spangler, a stagehand, was decorating the presidential box.[5] No one questioned Booth's right to be in the theater since he was familiar to all of the actors and other theater workers.

The bullet entered three inches behind Lincoln's left ear and lodged behind his right eye. The president slumped over, paralyzed, unconscious, and barely breathing.

The assassin dropped his gun and pulled out a dagger, a kind of sword. Major Rathbone lunged at him, but Booth

The assassination of President Lincoln on April 14, 1865, at Ford's Theatre is illustrated here. Major Rathbone is standing at left. His fiancée, Miss Harris, is to his right followed by Mary Todd Lincoln and President Lincoln (as the assassin fires the fatal bullet).

slashed deeply into Rathbone's arm, cutting it to the bone. Although the wound was not fatal, the pain was so severe, Major Rathbone could no longer hold on to the assassin. Booth tore free and leapt over the balcony. He caught the spur of his boot on the United States Treasury flag draped over the rail.

Booth fell to the stage below, shouting in Latin "*Sic semper tyrannis*" ("Thus always to tyrants"), which was Virginia's state motto.[6] He shattered a bone in his left leg, but he took advantage of the confusion that followed the shooting and escaped out the back door of the theater. Joseph Burroughs was waiting there with a horse.

At almost the same moment John Wilkes Booth shot President Lincoln, one of Booth's coconspirators, Lewis Paine (who was born Lewis Powell and also known as Lewis Payne and Lewis Wood) attacked Secretary of State William Henry Seward with a knife. Seward was in bed at his home recuperating from an accident at the time of the attack. Paine escaped, but not before he brutally slashed Seward's son and two other members of Seward's household when they tried to stop him. Paine fled and joined his partner, David E. Herold, who was waiting outside Seward's house with the horses. Paine told Herold their mission was accomplished. He was certain he had killed the secretary of state. In their escape, Herold and Paine were separated. Unknown to Paine and Herold, Seward survived the vicious attack (because he was wearing a metal neck brace as a result of an earlier carriage accident), as did the others who were wounded.

Two other planned attacks, one on Vice President

Lewis Paine, left, is on his way upstairs to kill Secretary of State William Seward when he meets Seward's son, Frederick, on the stairs. Frederick Seward was brutally slashed in the attack.

Andrew Johnson and another on General Ulysses S. Grant did not take place. The would-be assassin of Johnson, George Atzerodt, "lost his courage," and General Grant and his wife had already left Washington.[7]

Nine hours later, on April 15, at 7:22 A.M., the sixteenth president of the United States, Abraham Lincoln, was dead. This was the first time in American history that a president had been assassinated.

Booth Makes His Escape

Lincoln's assassin, John Wilkes Booth, made his getaway by cutting across Judiciary Square to Pennsylvania Avenue and riding south out of Washington. (Map of escape route shown on page 22.) Following closely behind was David Herold, who met up with Booth shortly after they had crossed the Navy Yard Bridge at the foot of 11th Street. There the bridge crossed the Potomac River. Although both men were questioned by a military guard, the guard was unaware that the president had been shot, and he did not stop either man.

In the days that followed, Booth and Herold traveled more than sixty miles by horse, canoe, wagon, and on foot through Maryland and Virginia. They stopped at various "safe houses," starting with the Surratt Tavern in Surrattsville (now Clinton), Maryland.

Mary Surratt's youngest son, John Surratt, Jr., was quickly linked with John Wilkes Booth as a conspirator by the Washington police. They may have known of his and Booth's earlier failed plan to kidnap the president in March, and came looking for John Surratt, Jr. just hours after Booth had made his escape.[8] But since they did not find young Surratt at home, they left without questioning anyone in the house. In fact, John Surratt, Jr. had apparently gone to Elmira, New York, before the attack on Lincoln. Later, he fled to Canada.

Booth and Herold's First Stop Is the Surratt Tavern

Booth and Herold arrived at the Surratt Tavern just before midnight. Booth downed several shots of whiskey provided by John Lloyd, the innkeeper who rented the tavern from Mary Surratt. Lloyd also handed over two guns that Mary Surratt, earlier that day, had instructed him to have ready for someone to retrieve. Because Booth was in great pain from his broken leg, he did not take the gun offered to him. Herold took the other one, as well as the field glasses left for Booth by Mary Surratt earlier that afternoon.

An artist's sketch shows John Wilkes Booth's escape out the back door of Ford's Theatre and up Baptist Alley.

Just before Booth and Herold left the tavern, Booth is said to have told Lloyd, "I am pretty sure we have assassinated the President and Secretary Seward."[9]

Lloyd, whose loyalties were to the Confederacy, did not rush to inform the police about his visit from Booth and Herold.

By early morning the two fugitives appeared at the home of Dr. Samuel A. Mudd several miles away. Dr Mudd was a Confederate sympathizer and had met John Wilkes Booth on several occasions, including one meeting that included John Surratt, Jr. Dr. Mudd set Booth's broken leg and made a set of crutches for him. Mudd would later claim that he had no idea that the man he treated was John Wilkes Booth. However, the boot, which he cut off Booth's foot, had the actor's name clearly written inside it. One day after Booth and Herold left, Mudd asked his cousin, Dr. George Mudd, to report that two "strangers" had been in his home on Saturday night.

Next, Booth and Herold stayed overnight in the home of Samuel Cox, another Confederate sympathizer. Then they were forced to hide out in the woods over the next five days in order to avoid the federal agents who, by then, were in hot pursuit.

On April 21, John Wilkes Booth wrote in his diary,

> After being hunted like a dog through swamps, woods, and last night being chased by gunboats till I was forced to return [to the woods] wet and cold, and starving. I am here in despair. And why? I am looked upon as a common cutthroat. . . . I struck for my country and that alone.[10]

After being turned away from some other hideouts in the days that followed, the two fugitives spent one night in a cabin on another farm. By now, their horses had become a burden. Booth and Herold barely had food for themselves. It appears that the horses were shot by Herold, although their remains were never found. With the help of Confederate sympathizers in Maryland and Virginia, Booth and Herold arrived at Garrett's Farm in Virginia on April 24. They were

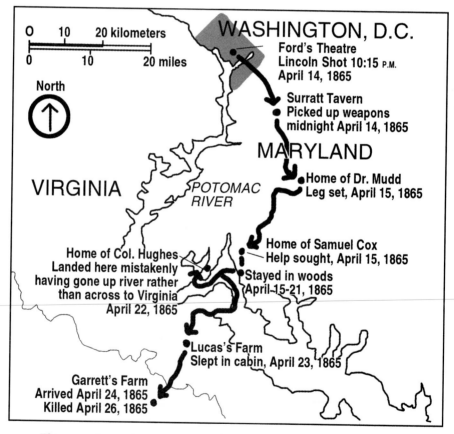

This map shows the escape route that John Wilkes Booth is reported to have taken following the murder of President Lincoln.

hungry, filthy, and ill from lack of sleep. Because the state of Virginia had seceded from the United States to become one of the eleven Confederate states, Booth believed that he and Herold would be safe. He expected to receive a hero's welcome for killing President Lincoln.

The United States Cavalry Finds the Assassin

In the meantime, Colonel Lafayette C. Baker of the United States Cavalry had received permission from Secretary of War Stanton to round up enough men to lead a search in Virginia for the two fugitives. Word had begun to filter back that Booth and Herold were somewhere between Stafford County and King George County in Virginia. Baker rounded up twenty-six troopers from the 16th New York Cavalry, plus a few more local men. The group soon learned that Booth and Herold were hiding in a barn at the tobacco farm owned by Richard H. Garrett.

On April 26, 1865, just twelve days after the assassination, Herold and Booth were discovered. Colonel Baker had his men surround the barn. He ordered them to hold their fire. Baker wanted to capture Booth and Herold alive.

Baker ordered the fugitives to come out. Herold obeyed and he was tied to a tree. John Wilkes Booth refused and raised his pistol.

Baker then ordered his men to set fire to the barn. Even as the flames engulfed the barn, Booth refused to surrender. As the fire spread, Booth, with his gun cocked, moved to the door ready to fire at his enemies.

Disobeying orders, one soldier, Sergeant Boston

Corbett, fired a single shot.[11] It was said to have struck Booth in the neck. Mortally wounded, John Wilkes Booth was dragged out of the barn. Lincoln's assassin died two hours later.[12] Colonel Baker had Booth's body secretly returned to the nation's capital. He was buried in the yard of the Washington Arsenal where four of his coconspirators would later die by hanging. There continues to be some controversy about whether Booth was shot by Corbett or if Booth committed suicide. Most historians accept Corbett's version.[13] Herold, who had surrendered, was taken to jail.

Mary Surratt Is Arrested

On the evening of April 17, 1865, just three days after the assassination of President Lincoln took place, federal agents arrived at Mary Surratt's boardinghouse. Unlike the metropolitan police who came looking for John Surratt, Jr., these agents had come to arrest Mary Surratt and everyone else who lived there. Mary Surratt's servant, Susan Jackson, had told the agents that on the night of the assassination, she overheard a conversation between two men and Mary Surratt.

Jackson reported that one of the men said John Surratt had been in the theater with Booth. The other man asked for a change of clothes.[14] It turned out that what Jackson probably heard was the conversation the Metropolitan police officers had with Mary Surratt, regarding the whereabouts of her son. Nonetheless, this was enough for federal agents to search the house and arrest Mary Surratt.

By this time, only the five women who lived in the house

were home. The two men, John Holohan and Louis Weichmann, had gone to the police the day after the assassination with some important information. They were already in what some would say was protective custody and others would claim was actual arrest. In fact, Lewis Weichmann was, at that very moment, in Canada assisting the Washington police in their search for John Surratt, Jr.[15]

When the women were rounded up and told the purpose of the visit by the authorities, everyone except Mary Surratt seemed surprised. One officer reported that Surratt took it all calmly, "as though she was expecting it."[16]

The federal officers searched the house and found what appeared to be evidence that the assassins had used the house as a meeting place. An envelope addressed to John Wilkes Booth at the National Hotel, where he had been staying, was found in Anna Surratt's writing portfolio.[17] A photograph of John Wilkes Booth was found hidden behind a picture on the mantel. Other items were also found.

Mary Surratt said she knew nothing of any assassination plans. However, just as it was nearing midnight, Lewis Paine,

Mary Surratt, shown here in the black veil she wore at her trial, did not seem surprised when police visited her boardinghouse following the murder of President Lincoln.

the man who had tried to kill Secretary of State Seward, knocked on Surratt's door. He was carrying a pick ax and was dressed in filthy clothes. A ragged piece of cloth covered his head. When asked his business, he claimed that Mary Surratt had hired him to dig a ditch. Surratt insisted she did not know who this man was, and that she had never met him before that very evening.[18]

But Paine had, in fact, been at Surratt's boardinghouse several times before the assassination. Much would be made of this fact at the trial. Even though the federal agents did not know who this man was, he was suspicious-looking enough for them to arrest him along with the others.

Mary E. Surratt was tried in a military court on charges of conspiring (joining in a secret plan) to murder President Abraham Lincoln, Vice President Andrew Johnson, Secretary of State William H. Seward, and General Ulysses S. Grant. Tried with her were David E. Herold, George A. Atzerodt, Lewis Paine, Michael O'Laughlen, Edman Spangler, Samuel Arnold, and Dr. Samuel A. Mudd. Mary's son, John H. Surratt, Jr., was named together with John Wilkes Booth as a conspirator in planning the attacks. Booth, of course, was dead. John Surratt, Jr. was in Canada where he was being hidden by sympathetic Catholic priests.[19] After his mother's conviction, he fled to England, and later to Rome, Italy, where he joined a group of men who guard the Pope. Jefferson Davis, president of the Confederate States, and "others, unknown," were also named in the indictment (formal charges of a crime).

Lewis Paine (left) is arrested. Federal agents did not know who he was but they found him suspicious-looking enough to arrest him.

The specific charges against Mary E. Surratt were as follows:

> Mary E. Surratt did, at Washington City, and within the military department and military lines aforesaid, on or before the 6th day of March A.D. 1865, and on diverse other days and times between that day and the 20th of April, A.D. 1865, receive, entertain, harbor, and conceal, aid and assist the said John Wilkes Booth, David E. Herold, Lewis Payne, John H. Surratt, Michael O'Laughlen, George A. Atzerodt, Samuel Arnold, and their confederates, with the knowledge of the murderous and traitorous conspiracy aforesaid, and with the intent to aid, abet, and assist them in execution thereof, and in escaping from justice after the murder of the said Abraham Lincoln, as aforesaid.[20]

Was the evidence against Mary Surratt that brought a conviction of treason against the United States by a military court really strong enough to warrant a sentence of death by hanging? Or was the enthusiasm of the prosecutors so intense in the aftermath of the murder of President Lincoln that evidence that could have proved Surratt innocent was overlooked? The answers to these questions have eluded scholars and assassination buffs for more than one hundred thirty-five years, and will undoubtedly continue to puzzle people for many more years to come.

Following the murder of President Lincoln, Ford's Theatre was draped in black.

chapter two

WHO WAS MARY SURRATT?

MARYLAND, 1823—Mary Elizabeth Surratt was born Mary Elizabeth Jenkins in June 1823, near the village of Waterloo, Maryland. She was one of three children, the only girl. Her father died when she was just two years old. But her mother saved the family estate, which included several slaves and a good deal of farmland. Mrs. Jenkins was an excellent businesswoman, and she soon was able to purchase even more land.

Jenkins also saw to it that her daughter received more education than most girls did at that time. Even though she was not Catholic, Mary Elizabeth was educated in a Catholic boarding school. While there, she converted to Catholicism.

In 1840, at age seventeen, she married John H. Surratt, who was eleven years older than she was. John Surratt was raised by Mr. and Mrs. Neale. He would inherit a large tract of land from them when they died around 1850. During that early period, John Surratt added more land to his holdings. However,

Mary Elizabeth Surratt was born Mary Elizabeth Jenkins in June 1823. She is shown here at age twenty-eight.

although he signed notes for several parcels of land, he rarely paid his debts.[1]

Nevertheless, John Surratt decided to build a tavern, attached to the Surratt home, which would also serve as an inn, and hopefully bring in some much-needed income. Unfortunately, Surratt would "become his own best customer at the bar."[2] Soon after it opened for business, the Surratt Tavern became a polling place at election time. Then the tavern was a designated post office. John was made postmaster and the village was named Surrattsville. These two appointments brought in a little money. In 1851, the home was destroyed by fire, but two years later, John had rebuilt it, along with the Surratt Tavern.

A Drunken Husband

Mary and John Surratt had three children, Isaac, Anna, and John, Jr. Mary Surratt tried to shield the children from their father's constant drinking.

According to letters written by Mary Surratt to her family and others, hers was not a happy marriage, because John drank heavily and was often in debt. In a letter to a Catholic priest dated January 17, 1858, Mary Surratt wrote,

> O, I hope Dear Father, you will try to get him [her son Isaac] something to do as it will be so much better for him to be out of sight of his Pa, as he is drunk almost every day & I fear there is little hope of his ever doing any better.[3]

In 1853, with debts piling up, John Surratt sold some of his land and in turn paid off a good deal of his debt. This land deal netted him $1,000 in cash as well as a townhouse at 541 H Street in Washington, D.C. Over the next eleven years, the Surratts rented out the H Street townhouse, while running the tavern in Surrattsville. But John Surratt continued to pile up more and more debt. So he sold off seventy-five more acres of his land to a man named John Nothey. Nothey, however, did not pay for the land all at once. John Surratt accepted a note from him.

Still, Mary Surratt did the best she could. As did her own mother, Mary valued education, and she managed to send her son John, Jr. to study at a Catholic seminary, St. Charles College. There he became friends with Louis J. Weichmann, another student. She sent her daughter, Anna, to Miss Winifred Martin's Catholic School for girls. Her oldest son, Isaac, had attended St. Thomas Manor, but when the school closed, he was sent to work in a shop in Baltimore. Mary Surratt was glad to have her children out of the house so that they would not be influenced by their father's drinking.[4]

The Civil War Tests Loyalty to the Union

By 1860, regional differences between the North and South were so pronounced that it was clear that war was inevitable. It was also clear that Mary Surratt and her friends were loyal to the South. Except for one of her brothers, "Zad" Jenkins, everyone else she knew supported either the Democratic Party nominee, Stephen A. Douglas of Illinois, or John C. Breckinridge of Kentucky, for president of the United States. Breckinridge, who was vice president, was the presidential nominee of the breakaway Southern faction of the Democratic Party. Zad Jenkins, however, was a staunch supporter of the Republican Party nominee, Abraham Lincoln, at least until Lincoln freed the slaves.[5] After that, his loyalty to the Union wavered.

In November 1860, Abraham Lincoln was elected president of the United States. In Prince Georges County where the Surratts lived, Lincoln received just one vote![6] In all probability, that single vote was Zad Jenkins's. (Mary Surratt, of course, could not vote, since women did not get the right to vote until 1920.) In all of Maryland, Lincoln received only 2,295 votes to Douglas's 5,873 and Breckinridge's 42,497.[7]

Maryland Stays in the Union

When the Civil War began in 1861, the people in Prince Georges County sided with the eleven Confederate states that left the Union. In fact, so did many of the citizens in other parts of Maryland. However, keeping Maryland in the Union was extremely important to the United States. If Maryland seceded, it would have meant that Washington, D.C., would be completely surrounded by Confederate states. President Lincoln simply could not let that happen. In fact, the Maryland state lawmakers voted to remain part of the Union only because federal troops had rounded up lawmakers who were Confederate sympathizers and jailed them before the vote took place. Even though many people thought this was illegal, President Lincoln knew it had to be done to keep Maryland firmly on the side of the Union.[8] There were two acts of Congress, one in 1795 and another in 1807, that authorized the president to call out the militia and use military and naval forces of the United States "to suppress insurrection against the government of a State of the United States."[9]

Mary Surratt's son Isaac immediately joined the Confederate Army and left for Texas. The tavern in Surrattsville soon became a center for Confederate activity. Confederate records list the Surratt Tavern as a "safe house" for Confederate spies.[10]

Mary Surratt Becomes a Widow

In August 1862, John Surratt died. Mary Surratt's son John, Jr. was forced to leave his studies at St. Charles in order to help out at the tavern. Union officials suspected that John, Jr. was involved in Confederate activities. They knew that his brother was a Confederate soldier. John, Jr., just eighteen, was dismissed as postmaster. This left Mary Surratt with very little income.

By 1864, Mary Surratt decided to rent the tavern to John M. Lloyd, a former police officer. He was to pay her five hundred dollars per year. She could then move to Washington. The house on H Street had been vacant for some time. If she could rent out some of the rooms there, she would be able to provide for her twenty-year-old daughter, Anna, and herself.

It did not take long for Mary Surratt to find lodgers. One of the first was John, Jr.'s old college friend, Louis Weichmann. Weichmann was living in Washington and was a clerk with the United States War Department. The others were Honora Fitzpatrick, age eighteen; Mary Appollonia

When his father died in 1862, John Surratt, Jr. (shown here) was forced to leave his studies to help his mother run the tavern.

Dean, who was just ten years old and attended a girl's school; and Mr. and Mrs. John T. Holohan and their two children, Mary and Charles. Other people came and stayed for a day or two or by the week. When John Surratt, Jr. stayed at the house, he shared a room with Weichmann. Another occasional guest at the H Street house was a young man named David Herold, who had once worked for a pharmacist near the Navy Yard in Washington. Others included a man who identified himself as a Baptist preacher named Wood, and a woman named Sara Antoinette Slater, a Confederate spy.[11]

John Wilkes Booth Meets Mary Surratt

On December 23, 1864, John Surratt, Jr. was introduced to John Wilkes Booth by Dr. Samuel Mudd.[12] Mudd and Booth were outside the National Hotel where Booth stayed when he was in Washington, when John Surratt, Jr. and his friend Weichmann walked by. Dr Mudd and John Surratt, Jr. had known each other previously, and the four men went to Booth's room after the introductions. Booth and Surratt, Jr. became friends. Booth would often meet John,

Dr. Samuel Mudd (shown here) introduced John Surratt, Jr. to John Wilkes Booth on December 23, 1864.

Jr. at his mother's house, and he sometimes brought along other people who were later identified as coconspirators. It was also known that Booth often met with Mary Surratt when her son was not home.[13] Mary Surratt would insist that Booth's visits were nothing more than social visits with a handsome and very famous friend of her son John.

But if Mary Surratt were simply an innocent landlady and good mother, why, as testimony would show, did she make at least two trips to Surrattsville, one of them just three days before the assassination and the other on the day of Lincoln's murder? On both occasions, she met her tenant, John Lloyd, even though she admitted that the person she wanted to see was John Nothey, who owed her money. Yet, on the second occasion Nothey was not in Surrattsville. Although he lived only a few miles away, Surratt did not visit him. Was her need to suddenly collect a thirteen-year-old debt the real reason for her trip? Or was it, as two witnesses would testify, to tell Lloyd that the "shooting irons" which were hidden in the tavern back in March by her own son John would be needed soon by someone?[14] And, on the day of the assassination, why did Mary Surratt deliver John Wilkes Booth's field glasses and tell Lloyd that someone would be by for them later?[15]

Mary Surratt did not make these two trips alone. She was accompanied by one of her boarders, Louis Weichmann, John's longtime friend. Weichmann was never named in the conspiracy, though. Both Weichmann and Lloyd would later testify against Mary Surratt at her trial. It was the testimony given by both these men, especially John

Lloyd, that would help to convict her. But if Mary Surratt was part of the conspiracy to kill the president, why did she travel with a person who could so easily be a witness against her? Did she believe that Louis Weichmann knew more than he really did? Was Mary Surratt just innocently doing a favor for her son's friend, John Wilkes Booth? Or was Mary Surratt the one who "kept the nest that hatched the egg," as President Andrew Johnson was quoted as saying?[16] In other words, was she the one who encouraged the conspirators to act?

chapter three

LINCOLN'S ENEMIES

EARLY WASHINGTON— Today, Abraham Lincoln is respected as, perhaps, one of the greatest American presidents. He is credited with keeping the Union together and with abolishing slavery throughout the land, although at the time he was first elected, his goal was not to abolish slavery, but to keep the country united.[1] His beautifully crafted speeches are studied by schoolchildren everywhere in America.

Virtually everyone who comes to Washington, D.C., visits the majestic Lincoln Memorial. Yet, even before he took office in 1861, many people feared that Abraham Lincoln might never serve as president. Many threats came from Southerners, who were already engaged in acts of war such as firing on ships carrying the American flag.[2]

In 1861, there were no such things as the Federal Bureau of Investigation (FBI) or the Central Intelligence Agency (CIA). Indeed, there was not even a police force in Washington. When the Civil War actually began, both North and South

Abraham Lincoln is shown here looking at a photo album with his son, Tad. Today, Lincoln is credited with keeping the Union together and with abolishing slavery.

had to quickly set up intelligence agencies. Many people thought that the South had the advantage when it came to spying—especially since there were so many Southern sympathizers already living in Washington.

The city of Washington organized its own metropolitan police force in 1861, but the one-hundred-fifty-member force was poorly paid and was not nearly big enough to patrol the city. Security for the president was lacking. There was no federal Secret Service until 1861. In fact, there was no White House guard or cavalry escort on the day President Lincoln was inaugurated (sworn into office).[3] Nor was President Lincoln properly guarded on the night of his assassination.

It was left to the War Department under the guidance of Edwin Stanton to organize security for the president and to seek out and stop spies.

There was, however, a private detective agency known as the Pinkerton Detective Agency. Its employees were hired to accompany large shipments of gold from the West to the East or to protect the mail as it was transported by rail across the country. Pinkerton detectives would ride the railroad cars to protect important passengers or important shipments of goods from bands of robbers. When Lincoln traveled from Illinois to Washington to be sworn in as president, Pinkerton detectives accompanied him because they had discovered a plot to assassinate him.

It was rumored that when Lincoln's train arrived in Baltimore, Maryland, where he would have to change to a different line, someone was ready to blow up his train. To protect his wife, Mary, President Lincoln was not permitted to ride on the same train with her. He had to change his plans and arrived in Baltimore late at night, wearing a disguise so that he could get to Washington a day early, undetected by would-be assassins. This plot has never been proven, although most historians do believe it was real.[4]

Not long after President Lincoln set up his cabinet, Secretary of War Stanton realized that there were Confederate spies everywhere. The Confederate Army knew many of the military plans of the Union Army. Stanton hired the Pinkerton Agency to identify the spies and arrest them.

Attempts Are Made to Kill or Kidnap the President

Just six weeks after Lincoln took office, a beautiful English actress named Jean Davenport, who was married to an American, arrived at the White House and asked to see the president. She was told he had already retired for the evening. She then explained to his aide that she had met a "dashing Virginian who . . . told her that he and six others . . . would shortly do something that would 'ring the world.'"[5] The man she named, a Mr. Ficklin, was never found. A few days later, someone turned up in Richmond, Virginia, and proposed to the Confederate secretary of war that it would be possible to blow up the Capitol at a time when the president and Congress were assembled together. Fortunately, nothing came of this plot, either.[6]

By 1863, with the war in full swing, Northern intelligence officers learned that a group of Virginia slave owners had formed a secret society to raise funds to be offered as a reward for anyone who killed Lincoln.[7]

Colonel Bradley T. Johnson of the Confederacy learned that the Union troops under Colonel Ulrich Dahlgren planned to carry out a raid to capture and kill not only the Confederate President Jefferson Davis but also his entire cabinet. Johnson was outraged.[8] Dahlgren's plans were spoiled by Colonel Johnson. He captured and killed Dahlgren and many of Dahlgren's men. Then Colonel Johnson planned to kidnap President Lincoln and bring him South, probably to Richmond. He thought Lincoln would be used as a bargaining chip to free Southern prisoners of war.[9] However, the kidnapping plot failed to materialize when the Southern army was stopped from entering Washington, D.C., at Fort Stevens, Virginia, just outside the capital.

According to historians James Lange and Katherine DeWitt, Jr., the first attempt to capture President Lincoln by a civilian occurred shortly after the failed attempt by Colonel Johnson. Captain Thomas Nelson Conrad, an ordained minister, received his orders directly from Jefferson Davis. He received money to run his operation from Judah Benjamin, the Confederate secretary of state. Conrad assembled a group of both civilians and military men and set up a spy operation just seven blocks from the White House.[10] Next, they occupied the home of a wealthy Southern sympathizer who lived just across the street from the White House. But Conrad abandoned his plan after six weeks of observation. He noticed that President Lincoln had started traveling with a guard. Conrad was afraid that

Lincoln's men were on to him, and he went back to Richmond to avoid capture.

Southerners were not the only ones who wanted to see Lincoln either dead or in the hands of the Confederates. There were Northerners who were in total sympathy with the South. Many Northerners believed that slavery was necessary (even sanctioned by the Bible), and that individual states could choose to leave the Union. One such group was known as the Knights of the Golden Circle. Its members were part of a secret group whose goal was to get states in the Northwest to secede from the Union.[11] One of its members was accused conspirator Michael O'Laughlen.[12]

In July 1863 there were massive riots in New York City to protest the forced recruitment of men into the army in what became known as the draft.[13] Many historians blamed these riots on the Knights. But others believe that a newer group, an offshoot known as the Order of American Knights, was behind the riots.

Another Northern group that hated Lincoln was known as Copperheads. Members considered themselves antiwar Democrats. They were called Copperheads because they wore in their lapels Indian heads cut from copper pennies. This organization, along with others, operated in both the North and South, and in Canada. Many fanatics had taken blood oaths to kill Lincoln.[14]

One of the most bizarre attempts to kill the sixteenth president involved a woman who disguised herself in widow's clothing and actually walked into Mr. Lincoln's office in the White House. Her aim was to kill the president with a poison kiss. Apparently she had a case of highly contagious and possibly lethal smallpox. The president *did* come down with a mild case of this disease in 1863, but it was not proven to be the result of the smallpox kiss.[15]

In 1864, plots to either kidnap or kill the president multiplied, especially after the South began to lose some important battles. One afternoon in August, while Lincoln was horseback riding on the grounds of the Soldiers' Home (about three miles from Washington, where Lincoln often went to relax), a shot rang out. The bullet went right through the president's hat. Lincoln made light of the event, saying he was sure that it was nothing more than an accident, rather than a sniper's bullet. He especially did not want his family to know about it.[16]

In December 1864, a Southern newspaper ran an advertisement offering a million-dollar reward to anyone who killed Lincoln, Secretary of State William Seward, and Vice President Andrew Johnson. If all three were killed, the United States would be in such turmoil that the South could easily win the Civil War.[17]

Colonel James Gordon of the Confederacy had a plan to capture President Lincoln. His account of what took place was published after the war, in 1891.[18] He said that while he was in Canada in March 1865 he met with John Wilkes Booth. By that time, everyone knew that the Confederacy was losing the war. They feared that President Lincoln would impose very harsh terms on the South. If Lincoln were captured and held hostage, perhaps the South could get better terms in a peace treaty.[19] But Colonel Gordon also said that at no time was he involved in any plot to assassinate the president.

Booth apparently had decided to try kidnapping the president the day Lincoln took his second oath of office, March 4, 1865, but quickly abandoned the idea as being too risky.[20]

On March 17, 1865, John Wilkes Booth and John Surratt, Jr., along with David Herold, Lewis Paine, and others, did attempt to kidnap President Lincoln. Their plan was to take Lincoln from Soldiers' Home to Richmond and hold him for a ransom of Confederate soldiers. This attempt failed because Lincoln remained in Washington.[21] Someone else was riding in the president's carriage. When Booth and his gang realized their mistake, they were certain that their plot had been discovered. Most of the men scattered—to Baltimore, New York, and elsewhere.

One can only guess how disappointed John Wilkes Booth was at having failed in his mission twice. He soon came up with a new plan—a

In December 1864, a Southern newspaper ran an advertisement offering a million-dollar reward to anyone who killed President Lincoln, Vice President Andrew Johnson, and Secretary of State William Seward (shown here).

murderous one. He bided his time. It would happen on April 14, 1865. He would bring down the United States government by murdering President Lincoln, Vice President Johnson, Secretary of State Seward, and General Grant. He had figured out just when the perfect moment for his attack would be. And he had lined up a number of conspirators to help him carry out his plans. Was Mary Surratt one of the conspirators?

chapter four

MARY SURRATT IS QUESTIONED

IN PRISON—Mary Surratt was brought to the headquarters at Old Capitol Prison on April 18, 1865. General Christopher Augur, commander of the Union troops in Washington, was the first person to question her. He was primarily interested in finding John Surratt, Jr. It was widely believed that he had been deeply involved in the assassination plot.

Mary Surratt insisted that she had not seen John, Jr. "since two weeks ago today, that is since the 3rd of April, 1865."[1] She did admit, however, that John Wilkes Booth had met John, Jr. about two months earlier, and that Booth frequently visited their home, even when John, Jr. was not there.[2]

When General Augur was finished questioning Mary Surratt, she was taken to the part of Old Capitol Prison known as Carroll Annex, where she was kept for several days without being charged. In the meantime, her daughter, Anna, was kept in the old part of

When she was questioned by the police, Mary Surratt acknowledged that John Wilkes Booth (shown here) frequently visited her home.

the prison and kept begging to be allowed to be with her mother.[3] It was not until May 11 that Anna was released from prison.[4]

On April 28, Mary Surratt was again questioned, this time by Colonel Henry Steele Olcott, special commissioner of the War Department. By then, three people had given sworn statements linking Mary Surratt to the events before and on the day of the Lincoln assassination. It had been confirmed that just before John Surratt, Jr. had tried to kidnap President Lincoln on March 17, John Wilkes Booth and his coconspirators had hidden two carbines (short, light rifles) and some rope under the upstairs floorboards at the Surratt Tavern. Once they grabbed Lincoln at Soldiers' Home, they were going to take him to the tavern and use the rope to tie the president up before taking him across the river to Virginia. They had even purchased a boat, which was hidden in Port Tobacco, Maryland, by George Atzerodt and kept ready for action. But Lincoln never went to Soldiers' Home on March 17. Instead the president attended ceremonies at the very hotel where John Wilkes Booth was staying.

John Surratt, Jr.'s friend Louis Weichmann and John Lloyd, the man who rented the tavern from Mary Surratt, both confirmed that Mary Surratt had made two trips to the Surratt Tavern, one three days before the assassination, and the other on the day of it. Colonel Olcott was interested in the conversations Mary Surratt had with John Lloyd.[5]

Finally, the maid, Susan Jackson, who lived with Mary Surratt, had given Colonel Olcott information about a conversation she overheard on the night of the assassination.

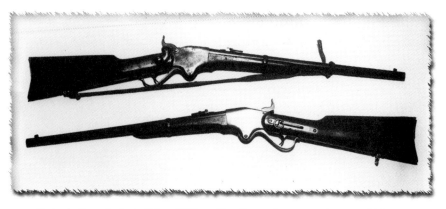

It is believed that John Wilkes Booth and coconspirators hid two carbines (short, light rifles like the ones shown here) and some rope under the upstairs floorboards at the Surratt Tavern.

Jackson claimed it was between Mary Surratt and two other men, one of whom was John Surratt, Jr. Colonel Olcott felt there was enough evidence against Mary Surratt to formally charge her with conspiracy in the assassination plot against President Lincoln.

Two Witnesses Are Needed to Prove Treason

In order to convict a person of conspiracy to commit treason (that is, trying to overthrow the government), it was not necessary to show that the person on trial actually pulled the trigger and murdered Lincoln. All that had to be proven was that the person took an active part in the conspiracy which resulted in the president's death. Anyone who was directly involved in any part of the plot shared the guilt equally.[6] According to the Constitution of the United States, it takes two witnesses to testify as to the guilt of the accused (Article 3, Section 3).

Colonel Olcott informed Mary Surratt that any statement she made to him would be used at her trial, although she did not have to answer any questions. But, he warned her, "You are a woman of too good sense not to know that it is better to refuse to say anything than not to tell the truth."[7]

Mary Surratt's answers contradicted the sworn statements of Weichmann and Lloyd. Of course, she had no way of knowing what they had said. Olcott was also interested in the whereabouts of John Surratt, Jr. (At least one newspaper claimed that Mary Surratt and her son would be pardoned if she would show the federal officers the road John, Jr. took when he escaped.)[8]

Mary Surratt insisted that John came and went as he pleased. She had not seen him since the week before the assassination. She showed her motherly concern. "I thought it better for him to be in Maryland than here where there were restaurants and bad company."[9] She denied knowing where John was because they had had an argument at dinner on Monday. He left the house with his friend Louis Weichmann. "When Mr. Weichmann came back I asked him where John was and he told me he had bid him good evening and said he was going away."[10]

Mary Surratt Visits Surrattsville to Collect a Debt

Colonel Olcott asked Mary Surratt about her two most recent visits to the Surratt Tavern. She replied she had received a letter from George Calvert, to whom she owed five hundred dollars as a result of her late husband's debts. Calvert wanted his money. Since John Nothey owed Surratt nearly the same amount of money for property he had bought thirteen years earlier, she decided to collect the money from him. Then she would pay Calvert what she owed him. "When I got there," she said, "I learned that Mr. Knothe [as Nothey's name was spelled in the records] . . . had gone to Marlboro."[11] So, she waited around for a while hoping that he would return, but he did not. She asked Weichmann to write a note to Nothey telling him she needed her money immediately.

Just as she was about to leave, Lloyd showed up. Mary Surratt would only say that their conversation was about food. Lloyd offered her "fish and oysters," but Weichmann,

When she was questioned, Mary Surratt described one of her visits to the Surratt Tavern (shown here on the left).

who had taken her to Surrattsville by horse and buggy, wanted to return home to eat. Surratt flatly denied saying anything about "shooting irons or carbines."

Colonel Olcott asked about other people who were involved in the assassination plot. Two other men stayed at her boardinghouse.

"Do you know a man by the name of Atzerodt or Port Tobacco?" (That was his nickname based on his hometown.)

"Yes sir. He came to my house to board. . . . He remained several days. . . . I found in his room bottles of liquor, and when my son came home I told him that I did not want this man to board; . . . I did not want him there."[12]

"You mentioned the other day that you had a man by the name of Wood, a Baptist minister in your house."

"Yes sir. He remained a few days."

Mary Surratt added that Wood came because he saw an ad for the room in the newspaper. She did not think that her son knew this man.

When asked if she recalled that the man who came to her house on the day of her arrest was, in fact, the man who had boarded with her, Mary Surratt answered:

"I do not. I thought he was calling for the gentlemen [the officers] there. I never noticed him."[13]

Mary Surratt insisted that she never thought the stranger at her door was the same person to whom she had rented a room a few months earlier. The light was very dim in the hallway, and her eyesight was poor.

Mary Surratt's answers did not satisfy Colonel Olcott.

She was indicted (formally charged) along with seven

others, as part of the conspiracy to commit treason by murdering Abraham Lincoln. The indictment was based not only on information given to the authorities by Louis Weichmann, John Lloyd, and others, but on the fact that many of the conspirators had lived in her boardinghouse. Especially significant was the fact that the man who confessed that he had attempted to kill Secretary of State Seward arrived at Mary Surratt's house at the very moment she was about to be arrested.

Many Women Acted As Spies

When Mary Surratt, her daughter, and one of Surratt's boarders were first placed in a cell on the second floor of the Old Capitol Prison, they found themselves in the same room with several convicted Confederate spies. Among them were Catherine Baxley and Rose O'Neal Greenhow and her daughter, "Little Rose." Greenhow was a daring woman, apparently much respected even by the guards. She was rumored to have helped Confederate General P.G.T. Beauregard win the first battle at Manassas.[14] Greenhow was captured by Alan Pinkerton of the Pinkerton Agency.[15]

It was a fairly common practice for the Confederacy to use women as messengers during the Civil War. And women were used as messengers by the North as well. In fact, Confederate General Braxton Bragg ordered the execution of Pauline Cushman who had been caught "behind Southern lines and condemned [to be shot] as a Union secret agent."[16] Her death was avoided only because Federal troops marched into Bragg's camp and saved her life. Another woman who spied for the North, Elizabeth Van Lew, was known as General Grant's "ace spy." She listened in on Jefferson Davis's war plans and reported back to the General. She was never captured.[17]

Neither the North nor the South liked to use the term "spy." Instead spies were referred to as "couriers," "scouts," or "agents." Needless to say, these people were considered heroes or traitors, depending on which side was the enemy.[18]

Many People Were Confederate Sympathizers

Before the Civil War, both Baltimore, Maryland, and Washington, D.C., were essentially Southern cities. The customs and social life of wealthy white families were modeled on those of the leading families throughout Maryland and Virginia. Many families were related by marriage and were sympathetic to the Confederate cause. Of course, they had to be very secretive about their politics.[19]

However, the Washington police knew of at least three secret meeting places where information could be exchanged. One place was the home of a woman known as Eugenia Phillips. Another was at a house near 7th and E Street, and still another was in Georgetown. Although the police could have broken up any meetings held at any one of these places, it was thought better to watch those houses and try to infiltrate them. But several rebel (Confederate) mail carriers were caught, while many others were kept under surveillance.[20]

Some people believed that Washington was full of

Some people believed that Washington, D.C., was full of Confederate spies. It was likely that Mary Surratt's boarding house (shown here as it looks today) was also kept under surveillance.

Confederate spies, and it was likely that Mary Surratt's boardinghouse was also kept under surveillance.

The North employed some very accomplished and colorful women spies, as well. Besides Elizabeth Van Lew and Pauline Cushman, there was Emma E. Edmonds. Edmonds was Canadian and was known to have made several trips behind Confederate lines disguised as a black laborer.[21]

Still, no matter how many women were actually caught in the act of spying for the enemy, no woman had yet paid with her life.

chapter five

THE TRIAL

MILITARY COURT—The eight prisoners charged in the assassination of Abraham Lincoln—Samuel Arnold, George Atzerodt, David Herold, Samuel Mudd, Michael O'Laughlen, Lewis Paine, Edman Spangler, and Mary Surratt—were tried together in the same courtroom. Because the nature of the crime—the murder of a president—had so shocked the nation, there were many rumors about who was responsible for the deed besides John Wilkes Booth and his confederates.

Many people in the North believed the assassination was the last desperate act of the Confederate leaders, namely Jefferson Davis, president of the Confederate states.[1] Various groups throughout the North passed resolutions calling for a swift and speedy trial. And in Washington, D.C., emotions ran so high that a mob of men attacked a man who said he was glad the president was dead. He was hanged from a lamppost and killed.[2]

Within the federal government there was

Many people in the North believed that the assassination of President Lincoln was the last desperate act of Confederate leaders, namely Jefferson Davis, president of the Confederate states.

suspicion that the Confederacy was deeply involved in the plot. And this suspicion was heightened when a letter was found in John Wilkes Booth's trunk. In the letter, he asked for a consultation with the Confederate government in Richmond, Virginia, and with supporters in Canada about the assassination of Lincoln.

On May 2, 1865, President Johnson issued a statement that

> it appears from evidence in the Bureau of Military Justice that the atrocious murder of . . . Abraham Lincoln and the attempted assassination of William H. Seward . . . were incited, concerted, and procured by and between Jefferson Davis . . . and other of the so-called Canadian Cabinet.[3]

Secretary of War Edwin Stanton insisted the prisoners be tried in a military court. United States Attorney General James Speed agreed that this was entirely legal. There were many reasons given for ordering a military commission to hear and to decide the case against the accused.

1. Although General Lee had surrendered to General Grant four days before the assassination, the United States was still technically at war. The final peace agreement had not yet been signed. The Constitution allows for military tribunals in time of war.

2. Martial (military) law was still in effect.

3. President Lincoln was commander-in-chief of the armed forces and therefore his murder was a military crime.[4]

4. The president of the United States has the right to require a military trial.[5]

Military trials were fairly common during the Civil War. President Lincoln was faced with states trying to secede from the Union when he took office in 1861. He had to act quickly and decisively if he were to preserve the Union. It was important not to let Washington, D.C., be surrounded by Confederate states. So he took away the right to a writ of *habeas corpus.* This is a court order to release a prisoner unless the government produces enough evidence to justify holding the prisoner for trial. Instead, the president instituted martial law, first in Maryland and Washington, and later, throughout the country.

In 1861 Congress passed laws

> approving, legalizing, and making valid all the acts, proclamations, and orders of the President . . . as if they had been issued and done under the previous express authority and direction of the United States Congress.[6]

In 1863, in the *Prize* case, the United States Supreme Court agreed.

War Powers of a President Are Limited

Not until 1867 did the Supreme Court of the United States limit the war powers of a president. In the case of *Ex parte Milligan* the Supreme Court ruled that a military court could not "supercede the civil courts in areas where the civil courts and government remained open and operational."[7] In the original case in 1864, Lambden P. Milligan, a citizen of

Indiana, who had never been in the military, had been sentenced to death by an army court for disloyal activities. Milligan had attempted to start an uprising in Indiana. President Lincoln had delayed his execution, pending an appeal. But after the assassination, President Johnson approved the sentence. Milligan's lawyers appealed his case to the Supreme Court. The Supreme Court ruled that since Indiana had not been under attack by the enemy, there was no reason for martial law to be imposed there. Furthermore, a civil court was in session, and martial law "can never exist where the courts are open. . . ."[8] If this decision had been issued before the trial of Mary Surratt and the seven others, they, too, probably would have been tried in a civil court.

Civil Rights Were Suspended During Wartime

Clearly, the cornerstone of the American Bill of Rights says that prisoners are entitled to a trial by a jury of their peers.[9] But the Civil War was a crisis of major proportions in U.S. history, and many of the civil rights people took for granted were suspended by President Lincoln at the height of the war. In 1861, the writ of *habeas corpus* (the "great writ" of Anglo-American law that provided for the release of people wrongfully imprisoned) was suspended.[10] President Lincoln used his war powers to limit other individual freedoms as well. He instituted a loyalty oath so that any male citizen who wanted to vote in an election, for example, had to take an oath of allegiance to the United States. Men were also required to carry official identification documents with them at all times.

Also in 1861, the president declared the country to be under martial law—that is law administered by military forces during a national crisis. Under martial law, more than thirteen thousand people were arrested on the mere suspicion of being blockade-runners, spies, or offering aid and comfort to the enemy.[11] Many people spent months in jail without ever being charged with a crime. Often, people who were charged were given military trials with the approval of United States Attorney General James Speed, who said, "The military tribunal exists under and according to the Constitution in time of war."[12]

Benjamin Perley Poore, a reporter for the *Washington Chronicle*, who covered the Surratt trial, wrote,

> The assassination of Abraham Lincoln was a military crime. While actually in command of the national forces, he was killed in a city which was his headquarters, strongly fortified and garrisoned with a military governor . . . not only was the murdered commander-in-chief, to use the words of the Constitution, "in actual service in time of war," but it was a time of "public danger."[13]

However, there were many people who were outraged that the defendants were ordered to be tried by a military tribunal. Their arguments were very powerful, but did not succeed. Among them were the following:[14]

1. Military courts can only try military offenses.

2. Civil courts are the proper place for crimes committed by civilians.

3. Only Congress and *not* the president can authorize a military court.

4. The United States Constitution's Fifth, Sixth, and Seventh amendments provide for the protection of people accused of a crime.

A Civil Court Offers Special Protection

If Mary Surratt had been tried in a civil court, she would have had some protections she did not have in a military trial. For example, according to the Bill of Rights, any person accused of a capital crime would first have had to go before a grand jury. It is the grand jury that decides if there is probable cause to bring a person to trial.[15] Surratt and her fellow prisoners would have had an opportunity to know what each was being charged with and would have had time to obtain attorneys who could prepare a proper defense.

In fact, the eight people accused found out what the charges were on the day they were brought into court on

The military tribunal that presided over the trial of Mary Surratt and her coconspirators is shown here.

May 9, 1865. They had only one day in which to find lawyers to represent them. And finally, if they had been found guilty of conspiracy in a civil court, they would have had the opportunity to appeal the judgement. This was not allowed in a military tribunal. Only the president could review the verdict.

One thing Mary Surratt would not have been permitted to do in a civil court in 1865 was to take the stand in her own defense. This is because that right is not based on English common law—from which laws in the United States developed. The only state to permit defendants to testify on their own behalf at that time was Maine. Not until March 1878 did Congress pass laws that guaranteed that right in both federal and military courts.[16]

Mary Surratt's attorney, Senator Reverdy Johnson, made an eloquent plea to have his client tried by a jury of her peers, but he was overruled by the Judge Advocate John Holt and by the president of the United States.

Mary Surratt was able to find three lawyers to represent her. Senator Reverdy Johnson was the most experienced of the lawyers. Unfortunately for Mary Surratt, however, once his plea to have his client tried in a civil court was denied, he did not appear in court again until it was time for closing arguments.[17] Some people felt that he abandoned her. The two other lawyers, John Clampitt and Frederick Aiken, who stayed on to defend her, were very inexperienced. Although Aiken had been a reporter for *The New York Times* before becoming a lawyer, he had not had much courtroom experience. Clampitt was just twenty-six years old and had practiced law for a very short time.[18]

The military commission that would hear the case was made up of nine men, most of whom were war heroes; others had been close friends of President Lincoln. All had served with honor in the Union Army. Brigadier General John Holt was appointed Judge Advocate. Brevet Colonel H. L. Burnett and Congressman John Bingham assisted him.[19]

The Trial Begins

At first, the trial was held in secret. But newspapers across the country denounced this as unconstitutional. Three days after secret testimony was taken, the trial was opened to the press.[20]

On May 10, 1865, the court assembled, and the prisoners were once again brought into the courtroom. The men sat along a wall, on the west side, on raised seats.[21] Each man had both legs and arms shackled. The men had to wear black hoods over their faces, which could only be removed during the trial. The prisoners were not permitted to speak to each other. There was one uniformed guard for every two men. There were some reports that Mary Surratt was in chains at the trial, but her attorney, Frederick Aiken, reported in the *Washington Chronicle* that she was at no time put in chains in the presence of the court.[22] All during the trial, Mary Surratt sat apart from the men. She wore a black dress and her face was somewhat hidden by a black veil. During the entire trial, it was claimed, she kept her head bowed, resting it in her right hand.[23]

Out of respect for the fact that Mary Surratt was an "older" woman (she was forty-two), she had been given a large cell on the third floor of the prison and was allowed to eat her meals with her daughter who visited her each day. She also did not have to wear a hood over her face. Apparently she was also given better food than were the male prisoners.

An Associated Press reporter described each of the prisoners as they sat in the courtroom. Mary Surratt was called a

> stout, buxom widow fitting Falstaff's ideal—"fair, fat and forty"—though it is ascertained she is far beyond that period of life, having nearly reached her grand climacteric. She was dressed in black, and looked a little flushed, but we failed to notice that "cold, cruel gleam in her gray eyes" which some of the gentlemen of the press have attributed to them.[24]

Dr. Mudd was said to look "calm, collected and attentive." Samuel Arnold was decribed as "nervous . . . and constantly varying the direction of his looks—now glancing from face to face, then bowing his head upon his hands."[25]

chapter six

THE CASE AGAINST MARY SURRATT

COURTROOM—The trial of the accused conspirators would last from May 10, 1865, when the government first started to present its case, until June 10, 1865, when the defense finished calling witnesses. Four more days were used for the government's responses and then each lawyer for each defendant had an opportunity to plead for his client. After that, Special Judge Advocate John Bingham spoke for the prosecution.

It was a long and often tedious trial. More than 350 witnesses were called.[1] Several defendants could not find a lawyer to represent them. Two defendants, Samuel Arnold and Edman Spangler, had the same lawyer—Thomas Ewing, Jr. Dr. Mudd had two lawyers—Frederick Stone and Thomas Ewing, Jr. Frederick Stone also represented David Herold, and Walter S. Cox was the lawyer for Michael O'Laughlen. William E. Doster represented George Atzerodt and Lewis Paine.

Brigadier General Joseph

Holt, Judge Advocate General of the United States Army, headed the prosecution team. In addition, there was John A. Bingham, Special Judge Advocate, and Brevet Colonel H. L. Burnett, Special Judge Advocate. The military commission hearing the case was made up of nine men, all high-ranking Union officers. It was known as the Hunter Commission because Major General David Hunter was the leader of it.

Any of the three prosecutors, as well as any or all of the defense attorneys, could ask questions of the witnesses. It took a team of five stenographers, headed by Benn Pitman, to write down the testimony of so many people, and there is some disagreement about the accuracy of their work.

This drawing shows the courtroom scene as it appeared during the trial. The military tribunal sits around the table in the foreground. Mary Surratt (face hidden behind a fan on the far right) and the others accused sit behind the railing.

Benn Pitman was the cousin of Sir Isaac Pitman who invented the Pitman shorthand system. It was Benn Pitman who leaked some of the secret testimony to the press. After the trial, Pitman, at his own expense, published the trial testimony. He arranged it in a logical form, so that the testimony related to the prosecution and defense of each defendant. But at the trial itself, witnesses were called in no special order. Many of the topics covered were not related to the assassination. Some of the witnesses were later proved to have lied. Attempts were made to charge the Confederacy in terrorist plots, including germ warfare and poisoning the New York City water supply.[2] It was, however, the testimony of two people, one of whom Mary Surratt had treated as a son, that sealed her fate.

Louis Weichmann Gives Damaging Testimony

On May 13, 1865, the first witness for the prosecution was called to testify against Mary Surratt. Louis J. Weichmann said he first knew John Surratt, Jr. when they were students at St. Charles College in 1859. They both left the college in 1862. They met by chance again a year later, when Weichmann was already working in Washington as a clerk in the War Department. When Weichmann learned that Mary Surratt had opened a boardinghouse on H Street, he became a boarder there until the time of the assassination. He testified that not only were John and Mary Surratt on friendly terms with John Wilkes Booth, but that several of the defendants had either visited the Surratt house or stayed there for various periods of time.

Weichmann told of the times several of the accused conspirators were either staying at the Surratt boardinghouse or meeting with John Surratt, Jr. Also, Sara Antoinette Slater and Augustus "Gus" Spencer Howell, known blockade-runners for the Confederates, visited. On March 18 John Surratt, Jr., Slater, and Mary Surratt drove off into the country together. "Mrs. Surratt told me on her return that John had gone to Richmond with Mrs. Slater. . . ."[3]

The picture Weichmann drew for the prosecution was that both John Surratt, Jr. and his mother knew many of the conspirators quite well. He told of walking down the street on the evening of January 15 with John Surratt, Jr. and suddenly hearing someone call, "Surratt, Surratt." (The date of that encounter was later found to be December 23, 1964.) The man calling out for Surratt turned out to be an old friend, Dr. Samuel Mudd. "He and John Wilkes Booth were walking together," Weichmann testified.[4] (This testimony upset Dr. Mudd's lawyers, because Mudd swore he did not recognize Booth when he set his leg the day after the assassination.) The four men stopped at the National Hotel for a drink, but then Mudd, Booth, and Surratt held a private conversation in a passageway to which Weichmann was not invited. After that time, Weichmann testified, Booth often came to visit either John, Jr. or Mary Surratt often. "Their interviews were always apart from other persons," he testified.[5]

Weichmann pointed out Lewis Paine in the courtroom and testified that he had stayed at Mary Surratt's house on several occasions, although he had given his name as

"Wood" and said he was a Baptist minister. He thought it was strange that Mary Surratt would rent a room to a Baptist minister since she and her family were all Catholics. But one day Weichmann came back to his room to find both John Surratt and Paine sitting on his bed "playing with bowie-knives [long knives with a double-edged blade and a curved handle]. There were also two revolvers and four sets of new spurs."[6]

Weichmann also recognized the "prisoner Atzerodt" as someone who had been at the house "ten or fifteen times."

Two days later, Weichmann was called again by the prosecution to continue his testimony. This time, he told about events some time after March 4, 1865. Weichmann testified,

> [John] Surratt came in very much excited—in fact, rushed into the room. He had a revolver in his hand— . . . a four-barrelled [sic] revolver, a small one you could carry it in your vest pocket. I said, 'John, what is the matter? . . .' He replied 'I will shoot anyone who comes into this room; my prospect is gone, my hopes are blighted; I want something to do. Can you get me a job?'"[7]

A few moments later, Paine came in, also very excited, and also carrying a revolver. Then Booth arrived and the three of them went off to a back room, and after half an hour they all left, Weichmann testified.

Weichmann Is Cross-Examined

When Weichmann was cross-examined by defense lawyers, he admitted that Mary Surratt was always very hospitable, that she had many acquaintances and friends. "During the whole time I have known her, her character, as far as I could judge, was exemplary and lady-like in every particular; and her conduct, in a religious and moral sense, altogether exemplary."[8]

But, when cross-examined by Aiken, he added that yet another known spy had been in Mary Surratt's house. "They refused to tell me his name," he said. But finally John Surratt told him it was Augustus Howell, whom Weichmann soon found out was a spy. This was very disturbing to Weichmann, and soon after that, he spoke to Captain Gleason, a clerk in the War Office. "There is a blockade runner at Mrs. Surratt's; shall I have him delivered up?" Yet, he decided not to go further with this, because John Surratt, Jr. was his friend, and he hoped this would be the only time it happened.

Weichmann's friendship with John Surratt, Jr. ended, however, when he saw in the newspaper that the would-be assassin of Secretary of State Seward wore a long gray coat. Weichmann had seen Atzerodt wearing such a coat and thought he might be the assailant. That is when he told the police what he knew.

> My only object was to assist the Government. I surrendered myself because I thought it was my duty. It was hard for me to do so, situated as I was with Mrs. Surratt and her family, but it was my duty and so I have always regarded it since.[9]

Although there were some inconsistencies in Weichmann's testimony, the defense lawyers could not catch Weichmann in a lie.

John M. Lloyd Testifies

The second person called in the prosecution's case against Mary Surratt was John M. Lloyd. His testimony would prove to be even more damaging than that of Weichmann. He said,

> Some five or six weeks before the assassination of the President, John H. Surratt, David E. Herold and G. A. Atzerodt came to my house. . . . John Surratt then called me in to the front parlor and on the sofa were two carbines with ammunition; also a rope from sixteen to twenty feet in length and a monkey wrench. Surratt asked me to take care of these things and to conceal the carbines. . . . He showed me where I could put them underneath the joists of the second floor of the main building. I put them in there according to his directions. . . .
>
> On Tuesday before the assassination of the President, I was coming to Washington and I met Mrs. Surratt on the road, at Uniontown. When she first broached the subject to me about the articles at my place, I did not know what she had reference to. Then she came out plainer, and asked me about the "shooting-irons." . . . I told her they were hid away far back, and that I was afraid the house might be searched. She told me to get them ready; that they would be wanted soon. . . . Her language was indistinct, as if she wanted to draw my attention to something so that no one else would understand. Finally she came out bolder with it, and said they would be wanted soon.[10]

The next time Lloyd saw Mary Surratt was on the day of the assassination. This time she met him out in the woodpile and handed him something wrapped in a piece of paper. "I found them to be field-glasses. She told me to get two bottles of whisky ready and that these things were to be called for that night."

Later that night David Herold came to the house and shouted at Lloyd, "Lloyd, for God's sake, make haste and get those things." Lloyd said he gathered up the carbines, the whiskey, and the field glasses. Booth remained on his horse, but Herold came into the house and took the whiskey out to Booth. "They only took one of the carbines. Booth said he could not take the other because his leg was broken. Then as the two men were about to ride off, Booth said, 'I am pretty certain we have assassinated the President and Secretary Seward.'" Lloyd said he was very unnerved by this news.[11]

When questioned by Stone, Lloyd admitted that he was "right smart in liguer [sic] that afternoon [on the 14th] and at night, more so."[12] Nevertheless, he was not so drunk that he could not fix the spring that had detached from the axle of Mary Surratt's rented wagon.

Others Testify Against Mrs. Surratt

Although the testimonies of Weichmann and Lloyd were by far the most damaging against Mary Surratt, the officers who arrested her were very surprised by how she responded when they came to her door on April 17. Major H. W. Smith testified that when he announced that he had come to arrest her, she never asked why she was being arrested.

Even more damaging was when Paine came to the door and Major Smith asked Surratt if she knew this man and if she had hired him to dig a ditch. Smith asked her, "Do you know this man, and did you hire him to come and dig a gutter for you?"

She answered, raising her right hand, "Before God, sir, I

do not know this man, and have never seen him and I did not hire him to dig a gutter for me."[13] Major Smith added that Paine was standing "within three paces of her when she denied knowing him."

Captain W. M. Wermerskirch, who was with Major Smith, confirmed what Mary Surratt said when confronted with Paine. And when he was cross-examined by Aiken, Captain Wermerskirch described how he searched Mary Surratt's house and found photographs, papers, a bullet mold, and percussion-caps (small amounts of explosive powder in metal cups) in Surratt's room. These items seemed to show that Mary Surratt had knowledge of the assassination plan.

chapter seven

THE CASE FOR THE DEFENSE

TRIAL CONTINUES— With little time to prepare for her defense, and with the hasty and unexplained departure of Reverdy Johnson as the lead lawyer, Aiken and Clampitt chose the only defense open to Mary Surratt. They portrayed their client as a religious woman who would never have involved herself in a plot to assassinate the president of the United States. They also attempted to discredit the damaging testimony of John Lloyd. However, the first person called by Aiken did nothing to help Mary Surratt.

George Cottingham was a member of the team of officers who had arrested John Lloyd. Lloyd was held for two days and then questioned by Cottingham.

"Oh, my God, if I was to make a confession they would murder me!" Lloyd told him.

"Who would murder you?" asked Cottingham.

"These parties that are in this conspiracy."

Then, Cottingham testified, Lloyd told how Mary

Surratt told him to have the "shooting irons" ready on the night of the assassination. And, perhaps, even more damaging, when the men came to arrest Lloyd, Cottingham said Lloyd cried out, "O, Mrs. Surratt, that vile woman, she has ruined me! I am to be shot! I am to be shot!"[1]

Aiken was startled and totally unprepared for Cottingham's testimony. He demanded Cottingham tell the court about the conversation he and Cottingham had just days before, when Cottingham told Aiken a different story.

During their private conversation, Cottingham said Lloyd never said Mary Surratt told him to have the guns ready. But Cottingham replied that he was not under oath then, and he was now. He said he objected to the way Aiken questioned him that night.

> He wanted to pick facts out of me in the case, but that is not my business; I am an officer, and I did not want to let him [Aiken] know any thing either way; I wanted to come here to the Court and state every thing that I know.[2]

Try as he might, Aiken could not shake Cottingham's testimony.

A Different Story Emerges

The next witness, Mrs. Emma Offutt, told a different story. She was in the tavern not only when Mary Surratt came on the afternoon of the 14th, but also when George Cottingham came to arrest Lloyd. She testified that Lloyd was so drunk on that day that she had to help him to lie down. She said that for the past few months he was drinking more and more. When Cottingham came to arrest Lloyd, she did not hear

him at the tavern. "She gave me a letter for Mr. Nothey, and asked me to read it to him, which I did. I have personal knowledge of Mr. Nothey buying land from Mrs. Surratt's late husband." Mr. Gwynn also had personal knowledge that Mr. Lloyd "had been drinking right smartly" on that day.[6]

The letter that Gwynn brought to Nothey demanded that he repay the money owed to Mary Surratt within ten days or she would "bring suit against him immediately."

Nothey swore that he did, indeed, owe Surratt money and that although he had seen her on the Tuesday before April 14, he did not see her on the day of the assassination of the president.

Mary Surratt's brother, J. Z. Jenkins, swore that he, too, had seen the letter from Calvert demanding his money, and in fact, it was he who had figured out that, with the interest owed on the thirteen-year-old note from Nothey, that sum of money just about covered what was owed to Calvert. Moreover, on the day his sister came to Surrattsville, he saw her, and "she expressed no wish to see Mr. Lloyd, and she was on the point of going when Lloyd drove up . . . Lloyd was very much intoxicated at the time."

Jenkins swore that his sister was loyal to the United States government. "I have known her frequently to give milk, tea, and such refreshments as she had in her house, to Union troops when they were passing." And Jenkins said that he knew that "Mrs. Surratt's eyesight is defective."[7]

When cross-examined by Assistant Judge Advocate Bingham, Jenkins strongly denied that he had threatened a witness who might testify against his sister. "I disremember calling him a liar during the conversation," Jenkins testified. He also denied that he was disloyal to the Union. "During the revolution, I have spent $3,000 in my district to hold it to the Union, and during the struggle I have taken no part against the government," he testified.[8]

In fact, several other witnesses testified that Jenkins was a loyal Unionist, even hoisting the United States flag up after the battle of Bull Run (a battle in which the Union troops were defeated). Although one witness, upon cross-examination, conceded that after Lincoln's Emancipation Proclamation, which freed the slaves, Jenkins did not vote for Lincoln or for representatives who supported Lincoln.

Anna Surratt Testifies

Perhaps the most poignant testimony was that of Mary Surratt's twenty-two-year-old daughter, Anna. She tried to shift the blame from her mother and brother over to Weichmann. It was Weichmann, she insisted, who had asked Mary Surratt to allow Atzerodt to stay at the boardinghouse. "They were sitting in the parlor, and made several signs over to each other." And shortly after, Weichmann asked to have the man stay the night.[9]

As for the photo of John Wilkes Booth that was hidden behind a picture on the wall, Anna explained that the photo of Booth actually belonged to her—and that when her brother saw it, he demanded she tear it up and throw it in the fire. But she wished to keep the photo of the great actor, and so hid it behind a framed picture hanging on the wall.

Anna Surratt also swore that her mother had very bad

eyesight, especially at night. "She has often failed to recognize her own friends. She has not been able to read or sew by gaslight for some time past."[10]

By the time Anna Surratt finished her testimony, it was reported that she was close to collapse, and she appeared to be under great stress. This stress became more apparent as she continued her testimony, often giving answers that were not quite true, such as when the last time was that John

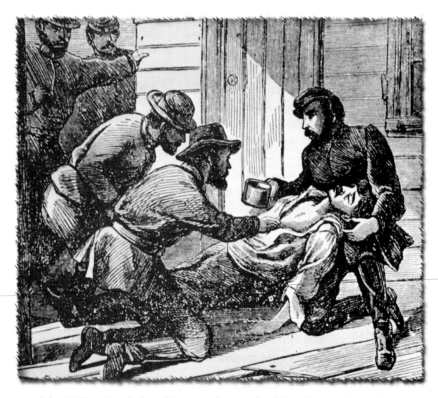

John Wilkes Booth lies dying on the porch of the Garrett home. Anna Surratt, Mary Surratt's twenty-two-year-old daughter, thought Booth was a great actor. She hid a photo of Booth behind a picture on the wall of their home.

Wilkes Booth came to the house. Her eyes kept darting around the courtroom in search of her mother, who was hidden from view by some spectators. It was reported that Anna's face was flushed, and her eyes filled with tears. At one point she asked, "Where is Mama?"[11] Colonel Douglas led her from the stand, and when she reached a room outside the courtroom, she fainted. She seemed to know that she had not helped her mother's case.[12]

Mary Surratt's Eyesight Is Questioned

Several witnesses testified that Mary Surratt's eyesight was failing. Honora Fitzpatrick, one of her boarders, said, "Mrs. Surratt has complained that she could not read or sew at night on account of her sight. I have known of her passing her friend, Mrs. Kirby on the same side of the street, and not see her at all." And when Fitzpatrick was recalled to the stand several days later, she said that she, herself, also did not recognize Paine when he came to the door on that night of April 17. "But I did at General Augur's office when the skull-cap was taken off his head."[13]

And then Fitzpatrick said that she often had to thread needles for Mary Surratt because her eyesight was so poor.

And although Eliza Holahan (or Holohan) also testified that Mary Surratt had very poor eyesight, she also testified that very often John Wilkes Booth came specifically to see Mary Surratt. "When he called he spent most of his time in company with Mrs. Surratt; he would ask for Mr. John Surratt, as I understood; if he was not there, for Mrs. Surratt."[14]

She Is a Lady and a Christian

Many people came to testify about Mary Surratt's character. Said Reverend B. F. Wiget, "I knew her and I have always heard every one speak highly of her character as a lady and a Christian."[15]

Other members of the clergy also came to her defense. The Reverend Peter Lanihan, who knew Mary Surratt for more than thirteen years, swore that she was "a highly honorable Christian woman, and had never said a disloyal word to him in their discussions about current affairs."[16]

His testimony was followed by that of Reverend N. D. Young. He said that Mary Surratt "was a lady in every sense of the word." Never had he heard a disloyal word pass her lips. In all, five members of the clergy spoke on behalf of Mary Surratt.[17]

Even former slaves spoke of Mary Surratt's gentleness and kindness to them and to strangers. John Hoxlen swore that "Mrs. Surratt's reputation is that of a truthful, kind and good Christian lady."[18] Another witness, also a former slave, Rachel Semus, testified that she was always "treated kindly; on one occasion Mrs. Surratt fed and took care of several Government horses that had broke out from the Government stables; she frequently fed Union soldiers."[19]

Despite the many strong character witnesses for Mary Surratt, her two lawyers could not produce enough evidence to discredit the damaging testimony of John Lloyd and Lewis Weichmann. The one person who might have been able to clear Mary Surratt was her son John, Jr. But he was in hiding in Canada and did not come to her rescue. It is not known if her oldest son, who was still in Texas, even knew she was on trial.

Closing Arguments Are Made

On June 10, the defense rested, and closing arguments began. Although Senator Reverdy Johnson did not return to the courtroom again, he did write at least some of the closing arguments. They were read by Aiken. Once again, he questioned the authority of the military court. He maintained that the proper place for this trial should have been in a civil court. The main thrust of his argument, however, was that Mary Surratt was accused of being part of the conspiracy merely because she had been seen in the company of other conspirators. "Now, in all the evidence, there is not a shadow of direct and positive proof which connects Mrs. Surratt with a participation in this conspiracy."[20] Aiken argued that there were only three pieces of evidence brought against Mary Surratt: her friendship with John Wilkes Booth, the message she supposedly gave to Lloyd regarding the "shooting-irons," and her failure to recognize Paine when he came to her door at midnight. These three things, Aiken argued, "are ordinary and commonplace." Even though Mary Surratt "received and entertained Booth, so did a hundred others. She may have delivered a message to Lloyd—so did a hundred others. She might have said she did not know Payne—and who within the sound of my voice can say that they know him now?"[21]

Aiken attempted, in his closing arguments, to throw suspicion on Lewis Weichmann, pointing out that it was

Weichmann who was invited to Booth's hotel room, "where he drank wine and took cigars at Booth's expense." And it was Weichmann who had introduced Atzerodt to Mary Surratt. It was also Weichmann who had invited Paine to remain in Mary Surratt's house another night.

Her lawyer portrayed Mary Surratt as "an innocent and guileless woman, not knowing what was occurring in her own house; . . . [when it was Weichmann who] was a spy and an informer."[22]

As for John Lloyd, he was so drunk that it was likely that whatever he remembered of his conversations with Surratt was unreliable. According to Aiken, Lloyd was one of the guilty ones, not Mary Surratt. Finally, however, the lawyer fell back on the testimony of those who identified Mary Surratt as a "proper Christian matron" who helped the poor, who fed Union soldiers, and treated her slaves with kindness. Such a woman, who on the very morning of the assassination went to church (because it was Good Friday), could not possibly be a person who would even think of taking part in such a heinous crime as the murder of a president.

The Prosecution Speaks

Judge Advocate Bingham spent a great deal of time arguing that the military tribunal was the proper place to try the conspirators, as he did at the opening of the trial. He argued that the president of the United States is the commander-in-chief of the armed forces; the country was still technically at war; the crime was committed in a city that was under martial law. He paid little attention to any of the arguments that the defense attorneys brought up, since Attorney General Speed had approved the military tribunal as the legal entity to try the conspirators. Bingham dismissed the speculations of Aiken that all the witnesses against Mary Surratt were the real conspirators, and that she was a simple, humble Christian widow trying to provide for her daughter and herself.

In fact, Bingham contended that "John Surratt and Mary E. Surratt were surely in conspiracy to murder the President as was John Wilkes Booth, himself."[23]

He conceded that Lloyd was a weakling and a drunk; nevertheless, he concluded his story was true. As for Weichmann, he was "a patriotic citizen who had done his best to support the Government and aid the forces of law and order."[24]

When Bingham finished, the case was over. The defense was not permitted to reply, and for two days the commission considered the evidence before announcing its decisions.[25]

chapter eight

THE VERDICT

THE DECISION—The commission announced its decisions on June 30, 1865. All eight defendants were found guilty of taking part in the assassination of President Lincoln. But the verdict was not made public until July 5, after President Johnson had had a chance to review the written decisions. Four conspirators, George A. Atzerodt, David E. Herold, Lewis Paine, and Mary E. Surratt were sentenced to death by hanging. Samuel Arnold, Michael O'Laughlen, and Dr. Samuel Mudd received a sentence of life imprisonment and hard labor. Edman Spangler was sentenced to six years imprisonment and hard labor.

Of the three men who were sentenced to hang, there was no doubt of their guilt. All three had confessed in writing. Somehow, however, George Atzerodt's confession had mysteriously disappeared, and would not be found until more than one hundred years later. Of the four sentenced to prison terms, Edman Spangler received the shortest term because his role in the assassination plot was minimal. Although neither Arnold nor O'Laughlen could be placed at the murder scene, Arnold seemed to have implicated himself and O'Laughlen in a letter found in John Wilkes Booth's room at the National Hotel. Many former slaves had testified against Dr. Mudd—that he routinely hid couriers and spies and was a Confederate at heart. Soldiers testified that Mudd had withheld information that he had harbored John Wilkes Booth and David Herold after the assassination. Weichmann's testimony that Mudd knew John Wilkes Booth was also damaging. Mudd, however, never confessed to being involved in the assassination plot. Nor did Mary Surratt ever issue a confession.

Five Have Second Thoughts

Curiously, although the commission condemned Mary Surratt to death, five of its members had second thoughts about her death sentence. In a separate letter, five commissioners recommended leniency for Surratt. They drew up a petition that asked President Johnson to find it in his heart to set aside the death penalty for Surratt "in consideration of her sex and her age" and, instead, to send her to jail for life.[1] Their recommendation did not suggest they believed Mary Surratt was innocent. They offered no reason why the commission had not given her a life sentence in the first place. They attached the paper to their verdicts and sent their reports to Judge Advocate General Holt. Holt kept them under lock and key in Secretary Stanton's War Department office until after July 4. The next day he met privately with President Johnson. From there, controversy arose. Did President Johnson read the memo signed by the five members of the commission? General Holt said that the president did. Later, President Johnson would deny he ever saw it. The only person who could commute Surratt's sentence (make her sentence less severe) was the president. President Johnson, though, maintained that he never was shown the petition for mercy. Judge Advocate Holt, however, said he was in the president's office and saw him read it.[2]

A Presidential Mystery Remains

When Holt returned to Secretary of War Stanton's office, he was asked what the president's decision was. Holt said that the president believed that if he did not agree that Mary Surratt should hang for her part in the conspiracy, "hereafter conspirators and assassins would use women as their instruments. It would be a mercy to womankind to let Mrs. Surratt suffer the penalty for her crime."[3] In other words, Mary Surratt's death would serve as a warning to American women. A woman who commits treason should not be given a lesser sentence simply because she is a woman.

The hangings were scheduled for July 7, 1865. On July 6, all the prisoners were told of their fate. Those who were to be hanged were informed as gently as possible.

Carpenters were hastily assembled and told to build a scaffold for four hangings in the courtyard of the Old Arsenal where the prisoners were held. But Major Eckhart, whose job it was to see that the task was done, said he believed that only three people would really hang. He, along with many others, did not believe that Mary Surratt would die. The three men—George Atzerodt, Lewis Paine, and David Herold, each of whom had made written confessions about their part in the conspiracy—asked to see family and clergy. Paine's father, who lived in Florida, never came.

The News Shatters Mary and Anna Surratt

The last person to be told of her fate was Mary Surratt. Her daughter had just left the cell when General John Hartranft told Surratt the verdict. The "tidings plunged her into a grief so profound as to excite the pity of the generals, performing a stern duty as they were."[4] Newspaper accounts reported that Mary Surratt burst into tears and proclaimed her innocence. She asked to see Reverend Wiget.[5]

Meanwhile, Surratt's lawyers were stunned and outraged to learn their client was to die. With less than twenty-four hours before the hanging, Clampitt and Aiken rushed into action. They met with Anna Surratt and together they approached Judge Advocate Holt to try to convince the president to spare Mary Surratt's life. Anna Surratt got down on her knees, imploring the general to intercede on her mother's behalf.[6] Holt gave in, and the three met him later at the White House. Aiken submitted what he claimed was important new evidence to prove his client's innocence. But when the lawyers and Anna Surratt arrived, Holt was just coming out of the president's office. He informed the trio that Johnson "saw no reason to change the date of the executions."[7]

A Glimmer of Hope Remains

Aiken and Clampitt telegraphed Senator Reverdy Johnson in Baltimore and begged him to return immediately to help them get a stay of execution (to have the execution postponed). But the attorney begged off. He suggested that it would be worth a try to get a writ of *habeas corpus* and then "take Mrs. Surratt bodily from the custody of the military authorities."[8]

Senator Johnson recalled the case of William Cozens in Philadelphia. He was a civilian arrested by the military who was issued a writ and given a civil trial. But was there a judge in all of Washington who would go against the decision of the military court and the president of the United States? It turned out there was.

Aiken and Clampitt finished writing their request in the early hours of the morning of July 7 and rushed to the home of Judge Andrew Wylie of the District of Columbia Supreme Court. Wylie was a man used to making decisions that were unpopular. At one time, he had lived in Virginia and was the only man in the state to vote for President Lincoln. One of his decisions while on the bench was to refuse to return a runaway slave to a Maryland owner during the war. Ironically, Lincoln's Emancipation Proclamation freed slaves in the Confederate states, but not in those states loyal to the Union. Wylie warned the two lawyers that he was putting his own life on the line by issuing the writ. But in truth, there was a great deal of respect for judges, and Wylie was never persecuted for his actions.

He issued the writ. At 4:00 A.M., a United States marshal

was sent with the writ to the prison officials to stop the execution.[9]

When President Johnson found this out, he immediately put an end to it, claiming that the writ of *habeas corpus* was suspended in this case, and the execution was to proceed as ordered. Johnson gave his message to Attorney General Speed, who took it to Judge Wylie. Wylie had to withdraw the writ.

Desperate Attempts Are Made to Save Her Life

Still, there were people who would not give up trying to prevent Surratt's hanging. Lewis Paine, in a moment of remorse, told both Reverend Wiget and General Hartranft that he felt responsible for Surratt's situation, since he appeared at her house at the worst possible moment. He swore she was not involved in the plot.

Both the general and Father Wiget wrote personal letters to President Johnson which they rushed to his office, begging him to stay the execution. Anna Surratt had made yet another attempt to see the president at the White House on the morning of the execution. But neither her tears nor her prayers would move the president's private secretary, General R. D. Mussey, to interrupt President Johnson. He had left strict orders that he not be disturbed. Newspaper reporters wrote that the general himself was moved to tears at the sight of the distraught daughter.[10] But President Johnson had made his final decision. David Herold's three sisters also came to the White House to plead for their brother's life. They were turned away as well.

This artist's rendering shows the conspirators as they are led to the gallows. Although Mary Surratt is shown here with her face covered by a hood, in reality, she was not hooded.

At 1:10 P.M., the prison cells were opened, and the four who were to hang were led into the courtyard. Mary Surratt was "clad in deep black. A serge bonnet from which depended a thick black veil, completely obscured every feature except the eyes. . . ."[11] The woman walked slowly, accompanied by two clergymen who "were constantly whispering faith to her. . . . She ascended the scaffold weakly, and was seated on a chair on the extreme left, the scaffold fronting southwest."[12]

At 1:26 P.M. on July 7, 1865, Mary Surratt, Lewis Paine, David Herold, and George Atzerodt were hanged. Mary Surratt's last words were "Don't let me fall."

The War Department sent Dr. Samuel Mudd, Edman Spangler, Samuel Arnold, and Michael O'Laughlen to a remote island prison called Dry Tortugas, seventy miles from Key West, off the coast of Florida. While they were in this prison, there was an outbreak of yellow fever. O'Laughlen died. In recognition of the lifesaving work Dr. Mudd performed during the outbreak, President Johnson pardoned him in 1869. In recognition of the lifesaving work that Spangler and Arnold had performed during that epidemic, they too were pardoned.

The hanging on July 7, 1865, took place in the yard of the penitentiary building. Mary Surratt is on the far left.

Decisions also had to be made whether or not to try other people named in the formal charges, especially Jefferson Davis, president of the Confederacy, who was in jail. It soon became clear that if Davis were to be tried for ordering the assassination of President Lincoln, he would be seen as a hero in the South.

And what of John Surratt, Jr., Mary Surratt's son? He was still in hiding. When would he be captured?

Many people wanted to put this terrible chapter in the history of the United States behind them and begin to repair the relations between North and South. The trial was over, and eight people had been convicted of conspiracy to murder the president of the United States. But there would be many difficult challenges ahead for President Johnson and the country.

chapter nine

THE AFTERMATH OF THE TRIAL

REACTIONS—Virtually all of the Northern newspapers applauded the death of the four conspirators and the long prison terms for the others. *The New York Times*, *The Baltimore Sun*, *The Boston Post*, and others all approved of the hangings of Paine, Atzerodt, Arnold, and Surratt. Several papers, including the *Baltimore Advocate*, said that the efforts to portray Surratt as a religious woman did not fit the enormity of the crime. Letters written to President Johnson were supportive of the decision to hang Surratt. In one, a Mrs. Dickinson wrote that she was satisfied with his decision without "yielding to sickly sentimentality . . . [which] would degrade the nation."[1]

One man wrote "I wish to say that your action in the case of Mrs. Surratt meets with approval. . . . Your action will teach bad women that government and men are not at their cruel mercy."[2] Southern newspapers printed the account of the hangings, but did not offer any further comments.

Not everyone, however, was content with Mary Surratt's fate. New information surfaced that seemed to cast some doubt on her guilt. Joseph P. Brophy, a friend of the Surratt family, went to a Washington newspaper, *Constitutional Union*, with an affidavit he had sworn to on the day Mary Surratt was hanged. In this sworn statement, he said that Louis Weichmann was a "liar" and a "coward." Brophy claimed that Weichmann told him that the reason he testified against Surratt was because General Holt and Secretary of War Stanton had threatened his life while he was in custody. Brophy also swore that Weichmann told him that Atzerodt was his friend. He also claimed that Weichmann knew that Mary Surratt did not know anything about what John Surratt and Booth were planning. It was John, Jr. who was the guilty one.[3] This article was reprinted in newspapers throughout the country.

Weichmann answered Brophy's charges in a letter to the editor of the *Philadelphia Dispatch*. He challenged Brophy's statements. After all, if they were true, why had he not testified for the defense at the trial.[4] And, in fact, most of the charges Brophy brought against Weichmann were answered while he was under oath.

Other people began to question how Mary Surratt was treated while in prison. *The New York Tribune* printed an article saying that one of Mary Surratt's "spiritual advisors," Father Walter, was told he could not visit with her "until he promised not to proclaim his belief in her innocence."[5] But, in fact, Father Walter had been granted a pass to visit with Mrs. Surratt. It was not until twenty-five years later that

This poster offering rewards for the capture of John Surratt, John Wilkes Booth, and David Harold, was posted following the assassination of President Lincoln.

Father Walter printed an explanation of the last conversation he had with Mary Surratt just hours before her execution. "Father, I wish to say something," she said. Walter replied, "Well, what is it my child?" "That I am innocent," she replied. Walter said that clearly these words were the . . . "last confession of an innocent woman."[6]

When the story of Anna Surratt's tearful visits to the White House surfaced, President Andrew Johnson was denounced as a tyrant and as Mary Surratt's executioner. It was said that when Mary Surratt's oldest son, Isaac, returned from his military service with the Confederate Army in Texas, his regiment buddies had encouraged him to "Go home and kill Andy Johnson."[7] President Johnson was soon labeled a "monster" and even worse names when it was learned that he had ignored the petition signed by five of the military commissioners that Mary Surratt's life be spared. President Johnson and Judge Advocate Holt were forever locked in furious disagreement over this.

Six months after the trial, the House of Representatives held hearings on whether or not Jefferson Davis and other Confederates had been part of the conspiracy to murder President Lincoln and others. A group known as the Radical Republicans was committed to punishing the South. Its members were unhappy with the conciliatory measures being put forth by President Johnson. These Republicans suspected Johnson of being a Confederate sympathizer.

However, witnesses who had testified at the original conspiracy trial, in which Jefferson Davis was named as the person who ordered the assassination, included a former

New York burglar with a long police record. Two other witnesses admitted they made up a story that they had overheard Davis and his secretary of state approve the assassination. A Confederate deserter was a convicted horse thief. Many others told the House committee they had lied under oath. The star witness, Sanford Conover, proved to be a complete fraud. He fled to Canada before he was captured. But he was eventually sent to prison for perjury (lying under oath). The entire case against the Confederates collapsed. Soon President Johnson was seen as a villain. The Radical Republicans gathered enough votes to impeach him (accuse him of misconduct while in office). Johnson became the first president ever to be impeached. He survived the impeachment trial in the Senate by just one vote and remained in office. But the Radical Republicans imposed very strict sanctions on the defeated South for the next two years, while President Johnson's influence as president was very limited.

Military Trials of Civilians Are Ruled Illegal

In 1866, less than a year after the trial, the United States Supreme Court issued a ruling on military trials in the case known as *Ex parte Milligan*. Lambden P. Milligan claimed that he had been improperly imprisoned in a military jail (where he was awaiting execution). He had been tried and found guilty of treason by a military court in his home state of Indiana. He claimed that as a civilian, he should have been tried in a civilian court. This right was guaranteed to him by the Constitution of the United States. The Supreme

Court agreed. It ruled that even when martial law is declared in time of war, "martial rule can never exist where the courts are open, and in the proper and unobstructed exercise of their jurisdiction. It is also confined to the locality of actual war."[8] Had this ruling come down before the trial of the conspirators, the eight accused might not have had the same sentences handed down.

John Surratt, Jr. Is Put on Trial

The *Milligan* ruling did affect the outcome of the trial of John Surratt, Jr. After his mother's death, John, Jr. slipped out of Canada using the name McCarthy. He got onto a ship bound for Liverpool, England. While on board the ship, he had many conversations with a physician. He told Dr. Lewis McMillan many things that he and John Wilkes Booth had planned, and finally he told Dr. McMillan who he really was. When the two men got off the ship in Liverpool, the physician went to the American consul and filed an affidavit in which he wrote down everything John Surratt had told him. The American consul immediately contacted the War Department in the United States, but Surratt fled first to France and then to Italy. Surratt went under another assumed name, John Watson. He got a job with the Pope's uniformed guard. One day, however, he was confronted by a man named Henri St. Marie, who remembered that the two had been introduced to each other in 1863. St. Marie reported Surratt to the American minister living in Rome, General Rufus King, who wrote to Secretary of State Seward. The chase was on to capture Surratt, who then fled to Egypt. He was finally captured and returned to the United States to stand trial for treason.[9]

John Surratt, Jr. was tried before a criminal court in the District of Columbia on June 10, 1867. Both John Lloyd and Louis Weichmann testified against him, as did Dr. McMillan and St. Marie. Surratt's sister, Anna, always loyal to him, sold pictures of him in his Papal uniform to raise money for his defense.[10]

Although it was John Surratt who was on trial, many people believed that this was really a retrial of his mother. Because the trial was held in a civilian court, it was very difficult for the prosecution and the defense attorneys to pick a jury of twelve men. There was still much hatred between Northerners and Southerners, both of whom resided in Washington, D.C. In addition, the jurors were limited to only white men. There were ninety-seven witnesses for the prosecution and eighty-five for the defense. There were bitter arguments between the attorneys, as the defense attorneys for Surratt tried to prove his mother was innocent. The testimony of Weichmann and Lloyd, however, did not substantially change, and in fact, Weichmann brought out new evidence against Mary Surratt.

The defense lawyer for John Surratt had a great deal of evidence indicating that John Surratt was not in Washington on the day of the assassination. This was meant to show that he could not have been involved in the plot to kill the president.

In the end, the jury was deadlocked. The jurors had deliberated for seventy-two hours and could not agree on a verdict. Judge George P. Fisher dismissed the jury that was made up of seven Southern-born men and five Northerners. The seven Southerners and one northerner had voted for acquittal (a not guilty verdict). Then the judge announced that the lawyer for John Surratt had threatened him during the trial. He told Joseph Bradley that he was no longer allowed to practice law in his court. "No court can administer justice, or live, if its judges are to be threatened with personal violence."[11]

John Surratt, Jr. was not tried a second time. Although he was indicted a second time for treason, Judge Fisher dismissed the case because the District of Columbia had a two-year limit on prosecuting most crimes. (Murder and fraud were exempt from that limit.) Surratt died on April 21, 1916, at the age of seventy-two.

Anna Surratt married Dr. William P. Tonry on June 18, 1869. Dr. Tonry, who had been employed in the surgeon general's office, soon lost his job. The couple moved to Baltimore, where Dr. Tonry established his own laboratory. Anna died on October 24, 1904.

John Lloyd continued drinking. He worked off and on as a bricklayer in Washington. On December 18, 1892, he fell from a building where he was working. When he died, he was buried in the same cemetery as Mary Surratt, where eventually Anna and John, Jr. would also rest.[12]

Louis Weichmann spent many years being hounded by those who believed he had lied about Mary Surratt. He finally moved to Indiana, where his sisters lived, and started a business. Before he died, at age sixty, he asked his sisters for a pen and some paper, and he wrote, "This is to certify that every word I gave in evidence at the assassination trial was absolutely true, and now I am about to die and with love I recommend myself to all truth-loving people."[13] He died on June 2, 1907. At that time, no one except his sisters knew that he had written a detailed account of his side of the story. His side of the story did not come out until seventy-five years after his death. It was in the hands of his niece, Alma Murphy Halff, and was first published in 1974.[14]

General Holt spent much of his life trying to prove that he had shown the appeal to spare Mary Surratt's life to President Johnson. He lived to be eighty-six and wrote to his friends that "Andy Johnson was not only mean and cowardly, but fake."[15]

Were those responsible for the assassination of President Abraham Lincoln the ones who were punished? This question continues to puzzle us today. Just as there are many theories, some reasonable and some completely fabricated, as to who killed President John F. Kennedy, there are dozens of theories put forth as to who was behind the killing of Lincoln. Here is a sampling of those theories.[16]

Abraham Lincoln's wife, Mary Todd Lincoln, believed that Andrew Johnson was responsible. In a letter to her friend, Mary Orne, she wrote: " . . . that, that miserable inebriate Johnson, had cognizance of my husband's death . . . he had an understanding with the conspirators & they knew their man . . . As sure as you & I live, Johnson had some hand in all this. . . ."

Lincoln's death was a simple conspiracy organized by

John Wilkes Booth. This theory holds that Booth dreamed up this plot with a small band of coconspirators.

Lincoln's assassination was a Confederate plot. This theory is based on the coded letters found in Booth's hotel room and on a confession by Atzerodt in which he told of Booth's knowledge of a Confederate plot. In their book, *Come Retribution*, authors William A. Tidwell, James O. Hall, and David Winfred Gaddy detail the work of the Confederate Secret Service in the plot to kill Lincoln.

The assassination was the result of powerful international bankers, and John Wilkes Booth was a hired gun. This theory came to light in an article, "The Rothschilds' International Plot to Kill Lincoln" in the October 29, 1976, issue of New Solidarity.

The Roman Catholic Church was behind the assassination. In 1886, a former priest, Charles Chiniquy, wrote the book *Fifty Years in the Church of Rome*. He claimed that the Jesuits were behind the one-million-dollar reward Jefferson Davis was said to offer to the killer of President Lincoln. Some people try to portray all of the coconspirators as Catholics, but not all of them were Catholic.

A favorite theory is that Secretary of War Edwin Stanton was the real mastermind behind the assassination. In his 1937 book *Why was Lincoln Killed?* Otto Eisenschiml wrote that Stanton was against Abraham Lincoln's mild policies about punishing the South. This author makes much of the fact that Stanton refused to supply Lincoln with his regular bodyguard and warned Grant not to go to the theater that night.

Other theories pop up from time to time. The Copperheads are often blamed as are some Radical Republicans, the B'Nai Brith, the Knights of the Golden Circle, Major Rathbone, John Parker (the man who was supposed to guard Lincoln and left him unattended), even Mary Todd Lincoln. There seem to be enough conspiracy theories to match everyone's taste. But the most likely theories seem to be the second and third ones mentioned.

Did She Do It?

Was Mary Surratt guilty as charged? Or was she, as her defense attorneys claimed, only doing a favor for her son's friend? On one hand, there was a considerable amount of circumstantial evidence (evidence that seems to point to a conclusion, but cannot be proven). She met privately with John Wilkes Booth on numerous occasions. In fact, she made two trips to Surrattsville during the week of the assassination. The second trip took place on the very day that Lincoln was killed. Both Weichmann and Lloyd gave damaging evidence against Mary Surratt. Her house on H street and the Surratt Tavern were both known meeting places for Confederate spies and messengers.

On the other hand, many people suspected that Weichmann and Lloyd knew more than they admitted about the assassination plot. Neither man, however, ever admitted to telling lies about Mary Surratt. Indeed, while many people hold strong opinions about the guilt or innocence of Mary Surratt, the truth remains buried along with her.

Chronology

April 10, 1865—Confederate general Robert E. Lee surrenders to Union general Ulysses S. Grant at Appomattox, Virginia, thus bringing to a close the Civil War between the Union States and the Confederate states.

April 14, 1865—John Wilkes Booth assassinates President Abraham Lincoln. Booth and David Herold flee Washington and stop at Surratt Tavern to pick up carbines and whiskey. Lewis Paine's attempt to assassinate Secretary of State William Seward fails.

April 15, 1865—President Abraham Lincoln dies and the country is plunged into deep mourning. Detectives search for John Surratt, Jr. Booth and Herold stop at Dr. Samuel Mudd's house for medical help. Detectives visit the home of Mary Surratt on H Street searching for her son. They leave when they find he is not there.

April 17, 1865—Federal officials visit the home of Mary Surratt. They search her house and arrest her, her daughter, Anna, and several female boarders. Lewis Paine appears at her door at midnight. He claims Mary Surratt hired him for some work. Surratt denies knowing him.

April 19, 1865—Edman Spangler is arrested. The funeral for Abraham Lincoln is held in Washington, D. C.

April 24, 1865—Dr. Samuel Mudd is arrested.

April 26, 1865—David Herold is arrested at Garrett's Farm in Virginia. John Wilkes Booth is shot and killed.

May 2, 1865—Six Southerners, including Jefferson Davis, president of the Confederacy, are named as conspirators in the Lincoln assassination.

May 6, 1865—President Andrew Johnson orders a military trial for the eight people accused of conspiring to murder the president of the United States.

May 9, 1865—The trial begins in secret. Newspapers and the public demand an open trial. The court agrees to allow access by the press.

June 30, 1865—A military court reaches its verdict. The verdict does not reach the desk of the president until July 5. Four people are to be hanged. Four people get prison sentences—three life sentences, one six-year sentence. Mary Surratt will be hanged, although five members of the military commission sign petitions asking the president to set aside the death sentence and reduce her sentence to life in prison.

July 6 and 7, 1865—Many people, including Surratt's daughter, Anna, plead for the life of Mary Surratt. The president refuses to meet with Mary Surratt's supporters. Lewis Paine tells a member of the clergy that Mary Surratt was not involved in the plot. Mary Surratt's lawyers get a judge to issue a writ of *habeas corpus.* President Johnson denies the writ. Mary Surratt, Lewis Paine, David Herold, and George Atzerodt die by hanging.

July 17, 1865—Dr. Samuel Mudd, Samuel Arnold, Edman Spangler, and Michael O'Laughlen are imprisoned on an island off the coast of Florida.

1866—The Supreme Court announces its decision in *Ex parte Milligan*. Civilians who are accused of treason must be tried in a civilian court if one is in session, not in a military court. The decision fuels the fire of those who believe that two of the convicted conspirators, Dr. Samuel Mudd and Mary Surratt, were unfairly tried.

November 27, 1866—John Surratt, Jr. is arrested. He is tried for conspiracy in a civilian court. The jury is unable to reach a verdict and Surratt is allowed to go free.

1867—Michael O'Laughlen dies in prison.

February 8, 1869—President Johnson pardons Dr. Mudd. Later that year, President Johnson pardons Samuel Arnold and Edman Spangler.

March, 1869—President Johnson allows the bodies of Mary Surratt and the others hanged to be released to their families. Lewis Paine's body is never claimed.

Chapter Notes

Chapter 1. A President Is Assassinated

1. Samuel Eliot Morison, *A Concise History of the American Republic* (New York: Oxford University Press, 1983), p. 624.

2. Guy W. Moore, *The Case of Mrs. Surratt* (Norman, Okla.: University of Oklahoma Press, 1945), p. 9.

3. National Archives, "Confession of Arnold," Washington, D.C., 1865, AGO roll 6 #541.

4. Otto Eisenschiml, *Why Was Lincoln Murdered?* (Boston: Little, Brown and Company, 1937), p. 54.

5. *The Trial of the Assassins and Conspirators for the Murder of Abraham Lincoln* (Philadelphia: Barclay and Company, 1865), p. 27.

6. Roger Norton, "Abraham Lincoln's Assassination," December 29, 1996, <http://members.aol.com/RVSNorton/Lincoln.html> (December 13, 2000).

7. Louis Weichmann, *A True History of the Assassination of Abraham Lincoln and the Conspiracy of 1865* (New York: Alfred A. Knopf, 1975), p. 6.

8. Eisenschiml, p. 41.

9. James O. Hall, *John Wilkes Booth's Escape Route* (Clinton, Md.: The Surratt Society, 1984), p. 6.

10. John Rhodehand and Louise Tapen, eds., "Right or Wrong, God Judge Me," *The Writings of John Wilkes Booth* (Urbana, Ill.: The University of Illinois Press, 1997), pp. 154–155.

11. Roy Z. Chamlee, Jr., *Lincoln's Assassins: A Complete Account of Their Capture, Trial, and Punishment* (Jefferson, N.C.: McFarland & Company, 1990), p. 189.

12. Sarah Mark, "Tracking the Assassin," *The Washington Post*, April 14, 1995, p. 14.

13. Chamlee, p. 290.

14. Ibid., p. 79.

15. Weichmann, p. 220.

16. Ibid., p. 80.

17. Chamlee, p. 81.

18. Elizabeth Steger Trindal, *Mary Surratt: An American Tragedy* (Gretna, La.: Pelican Press, 1996), p. 126.

19. Weichmann, p. 220.

20. Benn Pitman, *The Assassination of President Lincoln and the Trial of the Conspirators* (New York: Funk & Wagnalls, 1954), pp. 121–122.

Chapter 2. Who Was Mary Surratt?

1. James O. Hall and Joan Chaconas, *The Surratt Family and John Wilkes Booth* (Clinton, Md.: The Surratt Society, 1993), p. 3.

2. Elizabeth Steger Trindal, *Mary Surratt: An American Tragedy* (Gretna, La.: Pelican Press, 1996), p. 39.

3. Information courtesy of Surratt Museum Archives, Clinton, Md., 2000.

4. Trindal, p. 46.

5. Ibid., pp. 51–52.

6. Ibid., p. 8.

7. Bayly Ellen Marks and Mark Norton Schats, eds., *Between North and South* (Cranbury, N.J.: Associated University Presses, Inc., 1976), p. 17.

8. Bruce Catton, *Short History of the Civil War* (New York: Dell Publishing Co., Inc., 1963), p. 37.

9. Gerald Gunther, *Constitutional Law Cases and Materials*, 10th ed. (Minneola, N.Y.: Foundation Press, Inc., 1980), p. 414.

10. Trindal, p. 64.

11. Ibid., p. 101.

12. Ibid., p. 32.

13. Benn Pitman, *The Assassination of President Lincoln and the Trial of the Conspirators* (New York: Funk & Wagnalls, 1954), p. 133.

14. The Surratt Museum Home Page, © 2000 <http://www.surratt.org> (October 20, 2000).

15. Ibid.

16. Ibid.

Chapter 3. Lincoln's Enemies

1. Bruce Catton, *Short History of the Civil War* (New York: Dell Publishing Co., Inc., 1963), p. 20.

2. Theodore Roscoe, *The Web of Conspiracy* (Englewood Cliffs, N.J.: Prentice Hall, Publishers, 1959), p. 5.

3. Ibid., p. 10.

4. Ibid., p. 6.

5. William A. Tidwell, et. al., *Come Retribution* (Jackson, Miss.: University Press of Mississippi, 1988), p. 233.

6. Ibid., p. 234.

7. Ibid.

8. James E.T. Lange and Katherine DeWitt, "Who Ordered Lincoln's Death?" *North and South*, 1998, vol. 1, no. 6, p. 20.

9. Ibid.

10. Ibid., p. 21.

11. Bruce Catton, *This Hallowed Ground* (New York: Doubleday & Company, 1956), p. 268.

12. Roy Z. Chamlee, Jr., *Lincoln's Assassins: A Complete Account of Their Capture, Trial, and Punishment* (Jefferson, N.C.: McFarland & Company, 1990), p. 205.

13. Tidwell, p. 184.

14. Roscoe, p. 14.

15. Ibid., p. 10.

16. Ibid.
17. Ibid., p. 13.
18. Tidwell, p. 407.
19. Ibid., p. 409.
20. Chamlee, p. 114.
21. Ibid., p. 113.

Chapter 4. Mary Surratt Is Questioned

1. Roy Z. Chamlee, Jr., *Lincoln's Assassins: A Complete Account of Their Capture, Trial, and Punishment* (Jefferson, N.C.: McFarland & Company, 1990), pp. 566–567.

2. Ibid., pp. 567–568.

3. Elizabeth Steger Trindal, *Mary Surratt: An American Tragedy* (Gretna, La.: Pelican Press, 1996), p. 134.

4. Ibid., p. 147.

5. Chamlee, p. 184.

6. Ibid., p. 217.

7. National Archives and Records Administration "Statements Made by the Alleged Lincoln Conspirators Under Examination," (Washington, D.C., 1865), Microcopy-599, Roll 6, Frames 171–200.

8. "Editorial," *The Evening Star*, Washington, D.C., 1865, n.p.

9. Ibid.

10. Chamlee, p. 183.

11. Ibid.

12. Ibid.

13. Ibid.

14. Trindal, p. 132.

15. Theodore Roscoe, *The Web of Conspiracy* (Englewood Cliffs, N.J.: Prentice Hall, Publishers, 1959), p. 10.

16. Ibid., p. 489.

17. Ibid., p. 490.

18. Ibid., p. 13.
19. Chamlee, p. 57.
20. Ibid., p. 57.
21. Roscoe, p. 12.

Chapter 5. The Trial

1. Guy W. Moore, *The Case of Mrs. Surratt* (Norman, Okla.: University of Oklahoma Press, 1945), p. 28.
2. Ibid., p. 27.
3. Ibid., p. 29.
4. United States Constitution, Bill of Rights, Article V.
5. Janice Schuetz, *The Logic of Women on Trial: Case Studies of Popular American Trials* (Carbondale, Ill.: Southern Illinois University Press, 1994), p. 43.
6. Gerald Gunther, *Constitutional Law Cases and Materials*, 10th ed. (Minneola, N.Y.: Foundation Press, Inc., 1980), p. 414.
7. Civnet, "Ex Parte Milligan," © 2000 <http://www.civnet.org/resoures/teach/basic/part4/26.htm> (December 13, 2000).
8. Ibid.
9. United States Constitution, Bill of Rights, Article V.
10. Civnet, "Ex Parte Milligan," <http://www.civnet.org/resources/teach/basic/part4/26.htm>
11. Schuetz, p. 43.
12. Roy Z. Chamlee, Jr., *Lincoln's Assassins: A Complete Account of Their Capture, Trial, and Punishment* (Jefferson, N.C.: McFarland & Company, 1990) p. 52.
13. Philip Van Doren Stern, Introduction to the 1954 edition of Benn Pittman's, *The Assassination of President Lincoln and the Trial of the Conspirators* (Westport, Conn.: Greenwood Press, 1974), p. xviii.
14. Chamlee, p. 52.
15. United States Constitution, Bill of Rights, Article V.

16. Moore, pp. 34–35.

17. Thomas R. Turner, *The Assassination of Abraham Lincoln* (Melbourne, Fla.: Kreiger Publishing Company, 1999), p. 41.

18. Chamlee, p. 270.

19. Louis Weichmann, *A True History of the Assassination of Abraham Lincoln and the Conspiracy of 1865* (New York: Alfred K. Knopf, 1975), p. 85.

20. Chamlee, p. 31.

21. *The Trial of the Assassins and Conspirators for the Murder of Abraham Lincoln* (Philadelphia: Barclay and Company, 1865), p. 21.

22. "Letter to the Editor," *Daily Morning Chronicle* (Washington, D.C.), September 19, 1873.

23. Chamlee, p. 246.

24. *The Trial of the Assassins and Conspirators for the Murder of Abraham Lincoln*, p. 21.

25. Ibid.

Chapter 6. The Case Against Mary Surratt

1. Jill Meyers, "Context for the Trial Proceedings Documents," The Surratt Museum Web site, © 2000 <http://www.surratt.org/documents/dpitman.htm> (December 13, 2000).

2. Ibid.

3. Benn Pitman, *President Lincoln and the Trial of the Conspirators* (New York: Moore, Wilstach & Baldwin Publishers, 1865), p. 114. This is the official transcript of the case proceedings.

4. Ibid.

5. Ibid.

6. Ibid., p. 115.

7. Ibid., p. 118.

8. Ibid., p. 115.

9. Ibid., p. 119.

10. Ibid., p. 85.

11. Ibid., p. 86.

12. Ibid., p. 87.

13. Ibid., p. 122.

Chapter 7. The Case for the Defense

1. Benn Pitman, *President Lincoln and the Trial of the Conspirators* (New York: Moore, Wilstach & Baldwin Publishers, 1865), p. 124. This is the official transcript of the case proceedings.

2. Ibid., p. 125.

3. Ibid.

4. Ibid., p. 126.

5. Ibid.

6. Ibid.

7. Ibid., p. 127.

8. Ibid., p. 128.

9. Ibid., p. 131.

10. Ibid.

11. Roy Z. Chamlee, Jr., *Lincoln's Assassins: A Complete Account of Their Capture, Trial, and Punishment* (Jefferson, N.C.: McFarland & Company, 1990), p. 380.

12. Elizabeth Steger Trindal, *Mary Surratt: An American Tragedy* (Gretna, La.: Pelican Press, 1996), p. 182.

13. Chamlee, p. 132.

14. Ibid., p. 133.

15. Ibid.

16. Trindal, p. 177.

17. Ibid.

18. *The Trial of the Assassins and Conspirators for the Murder of Abraham Lincoln* (Philadelphia: Barclay and Company, 1865), p. 53.

19. Ibid., p. 51.

20. Frederick A. Aiken, Esq., "Argument in Defense of Mrs. Mary E. Surratt," in Benn Pitman, *President Lincoln and the Trial of the Conspirators*, p. 291.

21. Ibid., p. 293.

22. Ibid., p. 294.

23. Pitman, p. 346.

24. Theodore Roscoe, *The Web of Conspiracy* (Englewood Cliffs, N.J.: Prentice Hall, Publishers, 1959), p. 5.

25. Ibid., p. xxii.

Chapter 8. The Verdict

1. Roy Z. Chamlee, Jr., *Lincoln's Assassins: A Complete Account of Their Capture, Trial, and Punishment* (Jefferson, N.C.: McFarland & Company, 1990), p. 441.

2. Ibid.

3. Ibid., p. 444.

4. *The Trial of the Assassins and Conspirators for the Murder of Abraham Lincoln* (Philadelphia: Barclay and Company, 1865), p. 97.

5. Ibid., p. 97.

6. Chamlee, p. 457.

7. Ibid.

8. Ibid., p. 467.

9. Louis Weichmann, *A True History of the Assassination of Abraham Lincoln and the Conspiracy of 1865* (New York: Alfred A. Knopf, 1975), p. 85.

10. *The Trial of the Assassins and Conspirators for the Murder of Abraham Lincoln*, p. 98.

11. Ibid., p. 101.

12. Ibid.

Chapter 9. The Aftermath of the Trial

1. Andrew Johnson papers, "Dickinson to Johnson," July 8, 1865, Manuscript Division, Library of Congress, Washington, D.C.

2. Ibid., "Harris to Johnson," July 7, 1865.

3. Statement of Joseph B. Brody, Archives, Box 3, RG 153.

4. Louis Weichmann, *A True History of the Assassination of Abraham Lincoln and the Conspiracy of 1865* (New York: Alfred A. Knopf, 1975), p. 486.

5. Guy W. Moore, *The Case of Mrs. Surratt* (Norman, Ok.: University of Oklahoma Press, 1945), p. 65.

6. Reverend J. A. Walter, "The Surratt Case," *Church News* (Washington, D.C.), August 16, 1891.

7. Theodore Roscoe, *The Web of Conspiracy* (Englewood Cliffs, N.J.: Prentice Hall, Publishers, 1959), p. 490.

8. Civnet, "Ex Parte Milligan," © 2000 <http://www.civnet.org/resoures/teach/basic/part4/26.htm> (December 13, 2000).

9. Weichmann, p. 332.

10. Roy Z. Chamlee, Jr., *Lincoln's Assassins: A Complete Account of Their Capture, Trial, and Punishment* (Jefferson, N.C.: McFarland & Company, 1990), p. 517.

11. Ibid., p. 527.

12. Elizabeth Steger Trindal, *Mary Surratt: An American Tragedy* (Gretna, La.: Pelican Press, 1996), p. 182.

13. Weichmann, p. 405.

14. Ibid., p. xviii.

15. King Papers, "Horatio King to Thomas Harris," Box 13, Manuscript Division, Library of Congress, Washington, D.C., 1865.

16. Roger J. Norton, "Lincoln Assassination Theories: A Simple Conspiracy or a Giant Conspiracy?" January 20, 1998, <http://home.att.net/~rjnorton/Lincoln74.html> (December 13, 2000).

Glossary

acquit—To set free. To be found not guilty of a criminal charge.

affidavit—A written statement made under oath that is used as evidence in court.

closing arguments—The period in a trial after all the testimony for and against the defendant has been heard. During closing arguments, each side is permitted to summarize its case for the jury.

common law—Laws that the United States adopted from England, where they were supposed to reflect the customary rules of the people.

commute—To lessen an imposed criminal sentence.

Confederacy—The alliance of Southern states that attempted to set up a country separate and apart from the United States in order to maintain slavery.

conspiracy—A secret plan to commit a crime.

Copperheads—The name given to Northern Democrats who opposed Union policies and supported a negotiated peace with the Confederacy during the Civil War.

court-martial—The process used to try members of the armed forces.

cross-examination—Questioning of a witness at a trial by the opposing side.

deadlocked—A jury that is unable to reach a verdict.

defendant—The party in a case who is being charged with a crime.

impeach—To charge a public official with misconduct while in office.

inaugurate—To formally install a public official into office.

martial law—Military rule imposed when ordinary law is suspended.

perjury—Willfully telling a lie during testimony at a trial.

secession—The act of leaving. Eleven Southern states seceded from the Union during the Civil War.

treason—An attempt to overthrow the government.

Union—The name given to the twenty-three states that fought to abolish slavery.

writ of *habeas corpus*—From Latin meaning "you have the body." It is a document issued to a person under arrest to grant that person freedom. The government must have sufficient evidence to hold that person for trial.

Further Reading

Allen, William Francis. *Slave Songs of the United States.* Gretna, La.: Pelican Publishing Company, Inc., 1998.

Altman, Linda Jacobs. *Slavery and Abolition in American History.* Berkeley Heights, N.J.: Enslow Publishers, Inc., 1999.

Gaines, Ann Graham. *The Confederacy and the Civil War.* Berkeley Heights, N.J.: Enslow Publishers, Inc., 2000.

Hall, James O. *The Surratt Family and John Wilkes Booth.* Clinton, Md.: The Surratt Society, 1993.

———. *John Wilkes Booth's Escape Route.* Clinton, Md.: The Surratt Society, 2000.

Kent, Zachary. *The Civil War: "A House Divided."* Hillside, N.J.: Enslow Publishers, Inc., 1994.

Turner, Thomas R. *The Assassination of Abraham Lincoln.* Melbourne, Fla.: Kreiger Publishing Company, 1999.

Vandiver, Frank Everson. *1001 Things Everyone Should Know About the Civil War.* New York: Doubleday, 1999.

Varhola, Michael J. *Everyday Life During the Civil War: A Guide for Writers, Students and Historians.* Cincinnati, Ohio: Writer's Digest Books, 1999.

Zeinert, Karen. *The Lincoln Murder Plot.* North Haven, Conn.: Linnet Books, 1999.

Internet Addresses

The Lincoln Assassination

<http://member.aol.com.RVSNorton/Lincoln.html>

Lincoln Assassination Theories

<http://home.att.net/~rjnorton/Lincoln74.html>

National Archives and Records Administration— The Abraham Lincoln Assassination Report

<http://www.nara.gov/exhall/originals/lincoln.html>

The Search for the Real John Wilkes Booth by M. Christopher New

<http://users.erols.com/candidus/wilkes-1.htm>

The Surratt House Museum Home Page

<http://www.surratt.org/>

Index